M000039416

JONATHAN
PIE OFF THE RECORD

JONATHAN PIE OFF THE RECORD

TOM WALKER AND ANDREW DOYLE

Published by 535
An imprint of Blink Publishing
3.08, The Plaza,
535 Kings Road,
Chelsea Harbour,
London, SW10 0SZ

www.blinkpublishing.co.uk

facebook.com/blinkpublishing
twitter.com/blinkpublishing

Hardback – 978-1-911-60059-6
Ebook – 978-1-911-60060-2

A CIP catalogue of this book is available from the British Library.

Typeset by Envy Design
Printed and bound by Clays Ltd, St. Ives Plc

3 5 7 9 10 8 6 4 2

Every reasonable effort has been made to trace copyright holders of material reproduced in this book, but if any have been inadvertently overlooked the publishers would be glad to hear from them.

Blink Publishing is an imprint of the Bonnier Publishing Group
www.bonnierpublishing.co.uk

For Dad & Conrad

CONTENTS

ACKNOWLEDGEMENTS   IX

INTRODUCTION   XI

1   TONY BLAIR   1

2   KIM JONG-UN   17

3   MARGARET THATCHER   31

4   ADOLF HITLER   45

5   RUPERT MURDOCH   53

6   KING HENRY VIII   61

7   DAVID CAMERON   73

8   HARRY S. TRUMAN   95

9   SIMON COWELL   105

10 DONALD J. TRUMP   123

    CONCLUSION   149

    WHAT'S YOUR POLITICS?   151

    GLOSSARY   155

ACKNOWLEDGEMENTS[1]

I'd like to thank my two researchers Tom Walker and Andrew Doyle for their tireless research and never-ending dedication over the four and a half days that they were hired to work on the book.

I'd like to thank my wife's divorce solicitors (I think they're called something like Shotgun, Gluttony & Bastard Associates) for ensuring that she got practically everything in the settlement, making my financial situation almost untenable. Without such motivation, this book might never have been completed.

I'd like to thank my agent for allowing me the time to concentrate on my writing by not cluttering my diary

---

[1] This is a test footnote. The book is full of them, so get used to being interrupted mid-flow to look down at the bottom of the page for an amusing or irrelevant aside.

with after-dinner speeches, appearances on panel and quiz shows, or even putting my name forward to stand in for Matthew Wright when he's on holiday. Your fifteen per cent has been well earned.

I'd like to thank my producer Tim for his industrious hard work and patience. He is my rock.[2]

And I'd like to thank my family (what's left of it) for their unending support. Actually, my dad's support ended when he died and even before then it was perfunctory. I'm sad that he's not around to see my name in print. That said, he never seemed all that bothered that I was on the telly, which is a far more impressive achievement, so it's unlikely he would ever have read this book anyway. And who could blame him? I've written the thing and I'm fairly sure it's a bit shit.

---

[2] Gotcha, didn't I? You're a fucking dick, Tim. You're a fucking posh, ugly, talentless dick, and it's now here in black and white for the world to see which means that you are immortalised as a dick. (Must remember to delete this before going to press.)

INTRODUCTION

A Note From Jonathan Pie

POLITICAL CORRESPONDENT, JOURNALIST AND BROADCASTER

My publishers tell me that this book is officially what they call gift-able. A gift-able item. Mid-price light reading for the Christmas gift and merchandising market. Another popular term would be 'loo-read'. Or, if you're a pleb, 'toilet-read'. The implication being that this is the sort of book that is best enjoyed whilst poo is coming out of your bum.

I had never understood the idea of reading whilst taking a shit. 'Let's go and do a shit in the loo and then sit there reading a book or the latest *New Statesman* as I wallow in the aroma of my own dumps.' It seemed a bizarre choice when there's a perfectly good sofa nearby that doesn't smell of a combination of pine-scented bleach and faeces.

That was until my marriage began to fall apart. Then the lavatory became the only safe space in the house away from the constant eye-rolling and negative body language that is part and parcel of a relationship on the rocks. There I would spend many a pleasant hour with my trousers around my ankles, reading *Private Eye*, doing *The Guardian* quick crossword or simply sitting with my head in my hands, staring down at the worn, sweaty gusset of my underwear whilst wondering how to be a better husband, father, and all-round TV personality. Ever since then, and now in better times, I can fully appreciate the joys of a good loo-read.

All I ask is that any readers who insist on reading this tome on the lavatory, please make sure that the turd in question is worthy of a work of this calibre. I'm talking about a proper 'dad shit' that's halfway round the U-bend before it's even finished leaving your anus. One that is a struggle, that takes effort and time, but rewards patience. Just like this book.

I know what you're asking yourself right now. Is this entire book, all 178 pages, just about shits and arseholes? The simple answer to that question is: yes.

Because what follows are ten extensively researched chapters that deal with the people who have shaped our world, our politics and our lives. And they all have one thing in common. They're all either arseholes or utter shits. Often a combination of the two.

With that in mind, these pages are best absorbed soberly and thoroughly. This is why it might be best to save the book for those occasions where you are unable to leave your bathroom for most of the day. If, for example, you've eaten dodgy tapas.[3]

By looking at the lives of these ten awful twats you will learn about our history, our politics, our society and perhaps take a glimpse into the future. This book covers it all, from pig-fucking to pussy-grabbing. Part political commentary, part polemic, I hope it will leave you entertained, challenged, inspired and empowered, and that you will see fit to hand it down to future generations. [4] There's also a useful glossary at the back, which is a fucking godsend when trying to bump up your word count as the publisher's deadline is looming.

Enjoy.

JP

August 2017

---

[3] Indeed, I once had to step in at late notice for John Barrowman on some charity telethon or other (*Children with Needs*, I think it was called) after he ate some dodgy tapas on a cruise ship. He was by all accounts sat on the toilet for the best part of six days, but looked like a new man when he eventually emerged. He now regularly blocks out a fortnight from his diary to consume a strict diet that consists of raw chicken and milk that's on the turn. As John himself would testify, 'It beats jogging!'

My stint on *Children with Needs* was not my finest hour. However, footage does exist under the imaginatively titled *Jonathan Pie: LIVE!* and is available for download from my website for the very reasonable price of £7.99. Trust me, it's better than this book.

[4] Or, better still, buy the grandkids their own copy to enjoy.

TONY BLAIR

The Turd That
Won't Flush

Let me just set out my stall from the outset: I hate Tony Blair. I hate his smug rubbery smile and his cold, dead, soulless eyes. Most people these days hate Tony Blair. But I always did. I got there first. I win.

I hate the way we all went gaga for him when Diana died, how everyone went doe-eyed as he spoke to the nation and showed real emotion. Bollocks! He looked like a robot testing out a new grief algorithm. If he's capable of empathy, I've yet to see any evidence of it. I never voted for the man. It never even occurred to me to vote for him because his worst crime was committed before he even came to power. (Except for the small matter of causing over half a million deaths by taking us into an illegal war.)

The thing I hate the most about him is the fact that he destroyed the Labour party and all that it stood for. He took the best thing about British politics and fucked it. It was the political equivalent of giving the Sistine Chapel a once over with a Dulux roller. In short, he made left-wing politics popular again... by making it right-wing.

Only now Labour is beginning to return to its roots we can see just how bastardised the party became under Blair. Put simply, Blair and his curiously vampiric friend Peter Mandelson had created a new party and dressed it up to look like the old one. 'New Labour' was effectively a crafty euphemism for 'Not Labour'.

New Labour was like one of those annoying avocados that looks plump and enticing, but you cut it open and all you get is a massive inedible stone covered in a thin layer of green mush. Far from being the party of the people, New Labour was all about tackling middle-class problems. Such as sub-par avocados, for example.

So all that happened was that we replaced one Tory government with another, one that admittedly wasn't quite so toxic. It's like shifting from Marlboro to Marlboro Lights. It'll still kill you, but it'll just take a little while longer and it's more attractive to the kids.

Labour, from its early beginnings at the turn of the twentieth century, was about representing workers in parliament. The Liberals[1] had failed to help the working

---

[1] The Liberals were a major political party during the nineteenth and early twentieth centuries, and were the first to introduce welfare reforms. They were the main rivals of the Conservatives. They are not to be confused with the current Liberal Democrats, who aren't so much rivals to the Tories as a minor irritation that tends to self-destruct if left alone.

classes[2] and the Tories, true to form, simply didn't give a fuck about them. A new party was required to effect change, and so Labour was born. It was a union-led party that had socialism at its very heart.

But what exactly is socialism? Well, the technical definition is so fucking tedious that it's probably best restricted to a footnote.[3] But what it really boils down to is ensuring that working people have rights and aren't exploited by those in a capitalist society who have all the power. And the people with all the real power aren't the politicians. They're the fat cats, the snake-like CEOs slithering their way to the top, the Wall Street wolves ravaging the economy and rewarding themselves with huge bonuses and the corporate leeches sucking the lifeblood out of public services. It's basically a zoo of cunts.

In a socialist society, the government is there to ensure that wealth is redistributed and that individuals are taxed proportionately. It's a response to capitalism, really. It's not there to eliminate a free market, but to curb its worst excesses. Like when you have to secretly water down your nan's whisky because she's started banging on about 'them bloody wogs' again.

---

[2] The 'working classes' are best defined as those members of society who earn a low income from manual or industrial work. This is much more accurate than the more common definition of 'working classes', which runs along the lines of: people what read *The Sun*, eat at Greggs a lot and who love Ant & Dec's *Saturday Night Takeaway*.

[3] Socialism is defined as cooperative social and governmental ownership of the means of production and distribution, as opposed to a competitive free market system. There. Told you it was fucking tedious.

As you can imagine, socialism isn't popular with millionaires, because they *like* being millionaires. That's because millionaires get to have multiple yachts and villas in far-flung places where they don't have to interact with poor people, usually in a country where they don't have to pay tax. So it's in their interests to generate the myth that socialism is a destructive ideology, that the state helping poor people and those in need is not only a waste of money, it's downright unpatriotic. That homelessness, for example, is an acceptable and inevitable consequence of a healthy economy. Politicians and the media have been feeding us this shit for years, because, of course, most politicians and those who run the media are all fucking loaded.

So successful has this narrative been that by 1997, many Labour supporters considered socialism to be electoral suicide. Up until recently, most of the Parliamentary Labour Party felt the same way. But what really gets on my tits is that Labour is a party born out of the socialist movement. That's the whole fucking point. And yet Blair did everything he could to rid Labour of socialism. This involved a good deal of deception. And deception is one of Blair's specialities, along with killing Arabs, fellating US presidents, and I hear that he cooks a mean spag bol.

For those of you too young to remember a time before the Blair era, perhaps I can explain how he managed to hoodwink a nation into thinking they were voting for a progressive left-wing party. Well, Blair came out of the back end of the Thatcher years. As such he was, in effect, Thatcher's turd. But after eighteen years of a Tory government, the emperor from *Star Wars* would probably have seemed like a progressive candidate.

That's right. The Tories were in power for eighteen demoralising, humiliating, soul-destroying years before Blair came along.[4] No wonder the country was fucked.

Thatcher was long gone by the time Blair was on the scene but it's easy to forget that for the seven years before Blair entered Number 10, John Major was in charge. Easily forgotten because the man was instantly forgettable. He looked and sounded like an awkward nerd made of grey pipe-cleaners. He was notable for being the architect of the 'Back to Basics' programme to advance good old-fashioned family values, whilst at the same time secretly fucking Edwina Currie in the Cabinet Office (which is how Edwina playfully refers to her vagina).[5]

---

[4] A bit like the first eighteen years of my life, thanks to a dead dad and a mad mum.

[5] Edwina Currie is a former MP, novelist, reality TV star, and all round mad bitch. She caused a major national panic as junior health minister when she claimed that most of the country's eggs were infected with salmonella. It wasn't true, of course, but egg sales declined by a whopping 60 per cent. After that, fucking John Major doesn't seem quite so bad.

One of the reasons the Major/Currie scandal wasn't revealed at the time was that the nation was recovering from the mental image of another Westminster sex scandal involving the MP David Mellor sucking an actress's toes. (For those of you too young to remember, just google an image of David Mellor and imagine him erotically sucking your toes.)

Perhaps Major's relative invisibility is down to the fact that his premiership was bookended by two formidable characters: Thatcher the Milk Snatcher and Blair the Warmongering Shithead. To be fair to him, Major was the driving force behind the Northern Ireland peace process in those early years (even though Blair likes to take all the credit). He also fought to keep us out of the euro, which in hindsight was a great move. And, ultimately, he left the economy in pretty decent shape.

But after eighteen years of Tory rule, the country was looking for something fresh. People wanted change. The problem for Labour was they'd been unelectable for so long that they needed to change as well. It was time for Labour to find a new direction, to shake things up a bit. So the Labour leader at the time, a nice chap called John Smith, decided there was only one thing for it. He died.

Smith's passing left the top spot open for one of two contenders: Gordon Brown, a serious and well-respected politician and statesman; or Tony Blair, a grinning Cheshire cunt.

So the two of them went for a posh dinner in Islington where it was agreed that Brown was to become chancellor and Blair was to be PM. As part of the deal, Blair agreed that some day he would hand over the reins to Brown, but only at the right time. It turns out that what Blair meant by 'the right time' was 'when we are minutes away from a global financial crash that will undermine all of Brown's hard work as chancellor and make his new position as PM untenable'.[6] Classic Blair.

Under Blair, the Labour party won a landslide in the 1997 general election. He seemed amazing to anyone who couldn't see what an awful shit he was.[7] He spoke with an affected voice to conceal his privileged origins and the fact that he went to one of the poshest private schools in the country. He was young, photogenic and had boundless energy. He called himself 'Tony' rather than 'Anthony', and he used to be in a band! He also had a wife who looked like a frog, which was an intriguing novelty for a country that was used to the likes of Dennis Thatcher and Norma Major, who were far less amphibious.

We got so carried away with all the excitement that we forgot one crucial point. Tony Blair wasn't left-wing.

From the moment he was elected, all you had to do to be considered left-wing was read the *Guardian* and not use the word 'spastic' any more in polite conversation. An entire generation grew up thinking that being left-wing meant it was fine to sneer and hurl abuse at the working

---

[6] When Brown did eventually manage to get the keys for Number 10 he looked quite good for about ten minutes before going mad and hurling abuse at old women. In 2010, Gordon Brown was caught on a 'hot mic' referring to an elderly lifelong Labour voter, Gillian Brown, as a 'bigot' because she raised some concerns about immigration. It was a tactic that later become very popular with voters during the EU referendum in 2016. In a sense, then, Brown was something of a trendsetter. Years of disappointment at being in Blair's shadow had taken its psychological toll. Brown had transformed into a warped, paranoid angry bear which, to be fair, happens to many a frustrated middle-aged Scotsman.

[7] That's basically everyone but me.

classes and anyone who has a different opinion so long as you only use gender-neutral insults. Almost overnight, being left-wing became a middle-class hobby rather than a working-class necessity.

This fresh formula proved remarkably successful. Under Blair, Labour won its first hat-trick: three consecutive terms in office. But it was really a victory for what is known as the 'Third Way', which basically means neither left nor right, but somewhere in between. That's why they call it 'centrism'. It involves advancing lots of admirable values such as gay rights and equality for women, mixed in with insidious Thatcherite pro-corporate policies.[8] So whilst Blair held undoubtedly progressive views when it came to rights for minorities, he was also committed to fucking over the working classes. It's a toxic combination of right-wing ideology and left-wing virtue-signalling. Like beating a tramp to death with a rolled-up copy of *The Big Issue*.

In fact, Blair's upending of traditional Labour values was so pronounced that when Jeremy Corbyn eventually emerged as Labour leader he looked like a mad commie just because he was proposing basic socialist ideas. Whereas the truth is we'd all got so used to Labour behaving like Tories that we'd forgotten the difference between them.

---

[8] Bill Clinton also developed this 'Third Way' approach for the Democrat party in America, with a few notable variations. One of which was the introduction of fellatio into the Oval Office.

It wasn't until Corbyn became leader that Labour started moving back towards the left. The Blairites[9] were furious, and none more than Blair himself. Even now, he won't shut the fuck up about it. In one of his many interviews he attacked Corbyn, calling him a 'very dangerous experiment'. No Tony, Frankenstein's monster was a dangerous experiment. Jive Bunny was a dangerous experiment. Invading a Middle Eastern country on the basis of demonstrably inaccurate intelligence is a dangerous experiment. Having a socialist leader of a supposedly socialist party? Not so much.

So how did Blair manage to be so successful, given all that we now know about him? Well, it's an old-fashioned technique but it's one that definitely works. I believe the correct technical term is 'lying'. Blair is, and always has been, fundamentally dishonest. He lied about everything. He even kept his strong Catholic faith secret for his entire premiership. Doesn't it say something in the Bible about not bearing false witness? Clearly, Blair thought that God didn't really mean it. Although it was etched onto a stone tablet, which to me suggests a final draft.

The entire Iraq war, for example, was based on a lie. By taking us into the war under false pretences, Blair was

---

[9] A 'Blairite', as the word implies, is a devotee of Tony Blair. Otherwise known as a 'centrist' or, more accurately, a 'cunt'.

responsible for hundreds of thousands of deaths. Corbyn is responsible for – as far as we know – *zero* deaths. And Blair has the balls to say that Corbyn is 'very dangerous'. How fucking dare he call anyone 'dangerous', when we all saw him tear the Middle East to shreds only to leave office and make millions of pounds as a 'peace envoy' to the Middle East? He's either a complete psychopath or a comedy genius.

In the run up to the war, Blair soon picked up the nickname of 'America's poodle' because of his bizarre devotion to President George W. Bush. In many ways, the nickname is unfair. My uncle Edward has a poodle, but the worst thing she's ever done is piss on the eiderdown. To my knowledge, she hasn't ever instigated an illegal international conflict.

Bush used to say that he was standing 'shoulder to shoulder' with Blair. Well, they couldn't have been standing face to face because Blair's massive hard-on for Bush would've got in the way. He fucking *loved* him. He even wrote a memo to Bush in 2001 that reads like a love letter. 'I will be with you, whatever…' he writes. It's like some terrible Celine Dion lyric.

And it's bizarre, because Bush had a reputation for being the most sub-literate president of the century, paving the way for Donald Trump's gold standard of intellectual and linguistic flair. Bush once described Africa as a 'nation', and was quoted in the *New York Daily News* as saying, 'This foreign policy stuff is a little frustrating'.

Hardly reassuring coming from the man in charge of the nuclear codes.

So when Blair claimed that he'd seen 'firm evidence' of weapons of mass destruction (WMD), he was lying. And he was lying to the country and the world for one reason: to help his new best friend, George W. Bush. Not that it really mattered who was in the Oval Office. Blair had been sucking up to Clinton for years, and would've been the first in line to nosh off Donald Trump's little ginger penis if he had the opportunity. He wanted to crack America like The Beatles did, even if that meant going to war for no good reason. And nobody was going to stop him.

So what of Blair's legacy? In spite of ripping the beating socialist heart out of his party, and taking us into a needless war, he did achieve a few good things. He fought for a national minimum wage, made serious headway towards tackling child poverty, redressed legal discrimination against gay people, he left the NHS in a demonstrably better state than it had been (or has been since). And of course he worked tirelessly to ensure that John Major's work in Northern Ireland was continued and the Good Friday Agreement was carried through. All of which have been threatened by the Tories in recent years and months.

Unfortunately, it'll always be Iraq that is remembered

first and foremost. When you fuck up that spectacularly, it's bound to overshadow everything else.

But for me, it's what he did to the Labour party that makes him so contemptible. I don't want to see the man any more. I don't need to hear his whingeing about how the Labour party has moved too far to the left – you know, where it's *supposed* to be. I don't want to see him popping up all the time to give his opinions on politics, or the EU, or Jeremy Corbyn's leadership, or just about anything else that'll briefly restore him to the limelight. And yet he is never far away.

These are just a few of the reasons I hate this man. He is a warmonger. He is a neoliberal dressed up as a leftie. He is a liar and a cheat. He is definitely a narcissist and probably a sociopath.

I do realise that last comment is potentially libellous. But I'd happily spend what meagre savings I have left to enjoy the opportunity of proving it in a court of law. Bring it on, knob-end.

THE GREY BOX

Blair and the Chilcot Report

In 2016, the long-awaited Chilcot Report into the Iraq War finally surfaced, a 12-volume, 2.6 million-word overview of what went wrong. In response to the report, Tony Blair issued the following arse-covering statement: 'The report should lay to rest allegations of bad faith, lies or deceit. Whether people agree or disagree with my decision to take military action against Saddam Hussein; I took it in good faith and in what I believed to be the best interests of the country'. All this proved was that Blair hadn't read the report at all. He's probably still waiting for it to come out in paperback.

During the enquiry, Blair also insisted that he had done nothing wrong. The thing is, that's not up to him. It's now totally clear that he broke the law. He can't just *decide* that he didn't. That's not how it works. Criminals don't get to *decide* whether they are guilty or not. It'd make a mockery of the judicial system.

The report couldn't have been more damning. It concluded that Blair had been too quick to believe the flawed intelligence regarding WMD, and had made insufficient plans for the war itself or for the inevitable shitstorm that followed. In addition, the report judged that Saddam Hussein had presented 'no imminent threat', in spite of Blair's warnings to the contrary. It pointed out that the legal basis for war was unsound, that Blair had undermined the UN, and that his infamous 'dodgy dossier' had well and truly earned its nickname. Chilcot put it rather more politely, saying that when it came to assurances that Saddam was in possession of WMD, Blair's judgements 'were presented with a certainty that was not justified'. Or, to put it another way, he was talking out of his fucking arse.

How much does it take to get someone to apologise? Apparently a 2.6 million-word official condemnation isn't enough. Memos released at the time of the Chilcot Report prove that Bush and Blair had been discussing the removal of Saddam as early as 2001, just one month after the 9/11 attacks. This was his plan all along and, to put it bluntly, we shouldn't let the worm slither his way off the hook.

2

KIM JONG-UN

'The Democratic People's Republic of Korea is a genuine workers' state in which all the people are completely liberated from exploitation and oppression. The workers, peasants, soldiers and intellectuals are the true masters of their destiny and are in a unique position to defend their interests.'

Yeah, right. And two plus two equals five. What a load of bollocks!

The above quotation is from the official website of the North Korean government, which is weird because according to the North Korean state media the Internet doesn't actually exist. It's a fantasy invented by the West. And while it's strange that Supreme Leader Kim Jong-un feels the need to maintain a website for an Internet he doesn't believe in, when it comes to North Korea this is just the tip of a massive iceberg of frozen bullshit.

The word 'Orwellian' is bandied around a lot these days. You'll hear it in discussions about CCTV, the so-called 'Snoopers Charter', press regulation, or restrictions on freedom of speech. But the easiest way to understand what Orwellian really means is to take a look at North Korea, which is basically George Orwell's *Nineteen Eighty-Four* with an East Asian twist.[1]

Have you read *Nineteen Eighty-Four*? If you haven't, you're a cretin. Make the fucking effort. It's one of those novels that seems inaccessible, but is actually a great read.[2] And I'm honestly not very literary. I struggled with some of the more weighty Mr Men books. But *Nineteen Eighty-Four* is the fucking dog's bollocks.[3]

Orwell wrote *Nineteen Eighty-Four* in 1948 (see what he did there?) and predicted a nightmarish future in which an authoritarian one-party state controls the language, actions and, crucially, the thoughts, of its citizens. With the rise of Donald Trump in the US, and the Tories in power in the UK for so many years, it's worth reminding

---

[1] Imagine a bowl of grey porridge but with a dash of black bean sauce. But in book form. (This is a really tenuous analogy, isn't it? And possibly racist.)

[2] Except for Chapter Nine of Part II, which is admittedly a bit tedious. This is because it goes on and on in great detail about 'The Theory and Practice of Oligarchical Collectivism'. Seriously. Skip it.

[3] This is a serious recommendation. I mean, 80 million of you managed to read *The Da Vinci Code*, and that's a pile of utter horse cock.

ourselves that we're at least fortunate enough not to be living under a totalitarian regime. Donald Trump might be bad, but if I want to call him a half-witted orange sack of dildos I won't be dragged off in the middle of the night and 'disappeared' for doing so.[4] And when Kim Jong-un threatens the US with a 'pre-emptive nuclear attack', he makes Trump's tweets look like the very model of diplomacy.

North Korea was created in 1948, in the very year that Orwell's book was published.[5] There must be some massive cosmic irony at play here, but irony isn't really North Korea's forte (see their website for proof of this, which of course you can't because the Internet doesn't exist).

It all came about because of the Second World War. From 1910 until 1945 Korea was occupied by the Japanese. After Japan was defeated in the war (which is a nicer way of saying 'after Truman incinerated tens of thousands of their civilians'), the US assumed control of their territories. As usual in this kind of situation, they decided to arbitrarily split the country, leaving the north

---

[4] Although the Trump administration's systematic undermining of the press and penchant for 'alternative facts' is another fine example of Orwell in action.

[5] When the late journalist Christopher Hitchens managed to bribe his way into North Korea under an assumed identity, he said he was determined not to mention George Orwell in his write-up. Even though, as he pointed out, the 'schoolchildren are marched to school carrying pictures of the Dear Leader and the Great Leader. The loudspeakers speak of nothing but the Great Leader and the Dear Leader. At workplaces there are sessions set apart every day for cries of hatred against the United States and the West and South Korea.' Ultimately, Hitchens had to give in to using the word 'Orwellian'. Like he said, 'they make you do it'.

in the hands of the Soviets. This was always going to turn out well because historically, in states where civil conflict emerges, creating a new border has proven the most effective way of assuring stability. Oh, except for Ireland, Germany, India, and every other fucking place this has ever happened.

The Americans appointed an anti-communist leader to take charge of the south, which soon became a fully fledged democratic nation. The Soviets naturally wanted a communist to run the north, so they appointed a major from their Red Army, Kim Il-sung. There was just one problem: he was fucking mental.[6]

Kim Il-sung took no time at all setting up his Orwellian state. He dubbed himself the 'Great Leader', and reset the calendar so that it started in the year of his birth. That's why (at time of writing) North Korea is currently in year

---

[6] I know, I know. You're not meant to say 'mental' any more, are you? Or 'spastic'. Or 'mong'. It's political correctness gone mad.

Of course, I'm being facetious. The point is that language evolves and words fall out of fashion and can become offensive when faced with progressive attitudes. But often language too easily becomes the target of people's ire rather than the attitude itself, or the context within which the word was spoken. Those (typically left-leaning folks, it has to be said) who try to police language in this way are often well meaning, but you can't change someone's opinion simply by reducing the number of words available to express that opinion. A racist doesn't cease to be a racist just because he can't say the word 'Paki' any more.

In *Nineteen Eighty-Four* government officials attempt to control thought by controlling language. Specifically, by reducing the range of its citizens' vocabulary, it can reduce the range of ideas. For instance, 'good' is still a word in Newspeak, but 'great' and 'better' are not. Instead, you would say 'plusgood'. Words like 'excellent' or 'tremendous' are likewise outlawed, and can be expressed by the word 'doubleplusgood'. 'Bad' no longer exists, so instead you have 'ungood'. You get the idea.

Seriously, just read the fucking book.

105.[7] He also had statues of himself erected everywhere. And believe me, he was no pin-up.

The new regime saw its citizens as the property of the state, and since then it's only got worse. The government takes the role of 'Big Brother', which in Orwell's novel is the all-seeing eye that probes into every aspect of its citizens' lives. In the UK, we took the phrase 'Big Brother' and used it as the title for a mind-numbing reality TV show in which idiots live together in a fake house and are encouraged to humiliate themselves and suck each other off and shit in front of the cameras just for the chance of getting an interview in *OK!* magazine. It's like a Victorian freak show, only slightly more exploitative.[8]

But in North Korea, the 'Big Brother' concept has far more serious consequences than occasionally having to shower with Vanessa Feltz. Like in Orwell's novel, North Korean society is controlled by secret police who monitor the population's every move.[9] Torture, prison camps and executions are common methods by which the state

---

[7] The calendar isn't the only way they're out of sync. In 2015, Kim Jong-un had all the clocks permanently turned back by half an hour, because he claimed that the Japanese stole time from them during their occupation. It really is that mental. See footnote above.

[8] For a more in-depth look at our culture of exploiting the bewildered and talentless in a quest for mediocrity see the later chapter 'Simon Cowell: Britain's Got (very little) Talent'.

[9] The fear of punishment is particularly strong, because of the 'three generations' rule. If someone is convicted of a crime and sent to prison camp, they will be joined by their parents, grandparents and children. This, obviously, is massively fucked up.

keeps the people in line.[10] And if you're not seen to be praising the Supreme Leader with sufficient fervour, you are literally risking your life.[11] This is why 'Orwellian' is the most appropriate word.

Many people struggle to comprehend the leadership structure of North Korea, but it's actually pretty simple. The current president is technically Kim Il-sung, even though he died in 1994, and the government's General Secretary is Kim Il-sung's son, Kim Jong-il, who died in 2011, and the Supreme Leader is Kim Jong-un, son of Kim Jong-il and grandson of Kim Il-sung. I hope that's cleared that up.

But out of all these heads of state, Kim Jong-un has the unique advantage of actually being alive. You'll have seen him on the television. He's the one with a perfectly spherical head and the cheeky grin. He looks like an emoji, but one that you'd send to your ex-girlfriend if you were about to have her executed. Like Kim Jong-un did. Allegedly.

---

[10] In Orwell's novel, the torture chamber is known as 'Room 101', a place in which all your worst nightmares are realised. For us, it's a TV show in which Frank Skinner gets to chat to celebrities about what annoys them. This is usually things like umbrellas that won't open properly, or queues at the post office. And one that really boils my piss: Londoners who walk on the left on escalators but stop four steps before the end! Just fucking keep moving, you twat!

A North Korean citizen might have more legitimate gripes, such as state-imposed famine. But that wouldn't make such entertaining TV, I guess.

[11] When Kim Jong-il died, video footage of mass hysterical mourning in Pyongyang was seen around the world. The North Korean people were seen wailing inconsolably in front of the cameras. This, of course, was a true reflection of their sorrow at the passing of the man who had starved them nearly to death and killed so many of their friends and relatives. It had nothing whatsoever to do with the angry men brandishing guns in the background.

The confusion arises because Kim Il-sung, Kim-Jong-il and Kim Jong-un are all so similar that it's sometimes difficult to remember who is alive and who is dead. And it certainly doesn't help that the dead ones are still in office. That they're all called Kim isn't very useful either. I'm almost expecting Kim Kardashian to turn up as Minister for Fat Arses.

Moreover, if you look at pictures of the three Kims side by side, it's very easy to get them mixed up. Kim Jong-un actually had plastic surgery so that he would resemble Kim Il-sung. That's why it isn't racist to point this out. I'm not suggesting that all North Koreans look the same, I'm suggesting that all North Korean Supreme Leaders look the same.

This makes sense, because the dictatorship works on the basis of continuity. When one dies, an identical replica emerges, one every bit as deluded and megalomaniacal as his predecessor. And the current madman in charge of the country's nuclear arsenal, Kim Jong-un, is perhaps the most unstable of the lot. Fortunately, we now have Donald 'Mr Diplomacy' Trump in the White House, so there's very little to worry about.

Kim Jong-un is the master of the overreaction. He's a total diva. In 2015 he reportedly executed his defence chief for falling asleep during a meeting. He also had his uncle killed for philandering, gambling, and, wait for it, 'dreaming different dreams'. Illegal dreams! I'd get ten years' hard labour for that recurring one I have about Laura Kuenssberg with the strap-on and the tin of rice pudding.

The idea of criminalising certain dreams is the logical extension of the criminalisation of thought. In Orwell's *Nineteen Eighty-Four* you have the 'Thought Police', who arrest and torture anyone who thinks the wrong way. In this society, everyone must toe the party line. Those who do not hold the 'correct' opinions are to be silenced, and debate is a thing of the past.[12]

This is why Kim Jong-un can say whatever he likes and the population has to accept it. He can tell the people that when his father was born, the birds started singing in Korean, a giant double rainbow appeared in the heavens, a brand-new star appeared, and winter suddenly became spring.[13] In the West we might scoff at the very idea that any North Koreans would take this seriously, but that's all they've ever been told. It's no different from growing up in medieval England and believing that Jesus walked on water. Which, let's face it, lots of people outside of North Korea believe anyway.

The North Korean state media is the equivalent of Orwell's 'Ministry of Truth', whose slogans are simply the opposite of reality: 'War is Peace; Freedom is Slavery; Ignorance is Strength'. It's called 'doublespeak' – where you say the opposite of what's right in front of you. When the

---

[12] See the grey box.

[13] These events were so miraculous that the world's meteorologists were temporarily spellbound and totally missed it.

ministry insists that two plus two equals five, the citizens are obliged to accept it. Likewise, nobody in North Korea is going to challenge what the state media tells them is true.[14]

And so we get stories about how Kim Jong-il invented the hamburger,[15] how he could control the weather, and how he never had to use the toilet (this didn't stop him talking a load of shit, though). Most bizarrely of all, it is common knowledge in North Korea that Kim Jong-il was an international fashion icon. That's right, that guy who used to go around in a grey zip-up tunic and oversized sunglasses. Because apparently it's super-fashionable to dress like a recently divorced lesbian on a budget.

Even the official name of the country is a lie. If this truly is the 'People's Republic', why is it centred around the worship of one man? Why is it that the festively plump Kim Jong-un is able to live a life of opulence while the majority of the population don't have enough to eat? Indeed, the World Food Programme reports that seventy per cent of the population is malnourished.[16]

---

[14] There is even a fake propaganda village that they've built near the border with South Korea in order to give the impression that all is hunky-dory. Now that's commitment.

[15] According to the state media, when Kim Jong-il invented the hamburger he originally called it 'double-bread with meat', which perhaps isn't so catchy. But given the fact that hamburgers don't actually contain ham, it's as good a phrase as any.

[16] In the so-called 'demilitarised zone' between North and South Korea, the soldiers from each side stand face to face. North Korea chooses its most imposing men for the task, but the effect is somewhat marred by the fact that the average North Korean soldier is six inches shorter than his South Korean equivalent. The moral of this story is clear: if you don't want a stunted army, feed your people properly.

If it is 'Democratic', why is it that citizens must cast their votes not in private booths, but in full view of electoral officials? And why do all elections suspiciously result in 100 per cent approval for the Supreme Leader? Those are the sort of approval ratings that even Theresa May couldn't fuck up.

This is why Kim Jong-un's government are not being ironic when they issue statements through an Internet that doesn't exist. Of course North Korea is 'a genuine workers' state in which all the people are completely liberated from exploitation and oppression'. Because when your head of state is a dead god, when you can be tortured or killed for speaking your mind, and when you have to continually express your gratitude for the famine you're enduring at the hands of your Supreme Leader, who is to say that two plus two doesn't equal five?

THE GREY BOX

*Modern Universities: Our Own Little
Orwellian Nightmare*

University used to be a place to expand your
worldview, to exchange ideas and to debate robustly.
It also used to be the place you went if you wanted
to get pissed for three years on a low-interest
loan. Being a student used to mean a pound a pint
down the union. Now the NUS (National Union of
Students) is pushing to raise alcohol prices to curb
binge drinking. But this is just the tip of the shitberg.

What's happened to the NUS? Why has this vocal
and self-important minority been given the power
to impose 'safe spaces' to prevent the discussion of
difficult ideas? Why are they inviting speakers to their
universities only to disinvite them (or 'no platform'
them) for their supposedly contentious views? Isn't
contention the very point of debate? Trust me, this
is happening all over university campuses and it isn't
healthy.

In the aftermath of Donald Trump's election, sales
of *Nineteen Eighty-Four* rocketed because people
were attempting to understand his regime. And
although Trump's disdain for press freedom and

complete denial of reality does have an Orwellian flavour, it's often those on the Liberal-Left, who fear free speech and hate democracy when it doesn't go their way, who most seem to emulate Orwell's dystopian state. After they bought the book, I wonder how many of them saw themselves reflected in its contents? Students are meant to be like Rik from *The Young Ones*, not Mary fucking Whitehouse. It's a bizarre state of affairs when all this youthful energy is expended on stopping debates rather than trying to win them.

In *Nineteen Eighty-Four*, the Ministry of Truth has a 'memory hole', down which they deposit all documents, photographs, or other evidence of events that the state claims never happened. At the bottom of the memory hole is an incinerator. They literally eliminate uncomfortable elements of the past.

This kind of revisionism is now being embraced by some students in the name of 'tolerance'. There is evidence that art history lecturers are being encouraged to change the curriculum so as not to show any naked breasts for fear of causing offence to women or religious minorities. Look, you can't do art history without coming across some tits! (Sorry, that came out wrong.)

Great works of poetry and fiction are being edited out of the English curriculum for fear of causing offence. Bullshit. If you're offended by *To Kill a Mockingbird* because it uses language that is no longer considered acceptable, then you're a fucking idiot. If you're unable or unwilling to see things in their historical context, then you shouldn't be doing a fucking literature degree in the first place.

In *Nineteen Eighty-Four* (read it!) the protagonist Winston Smith is employed by the Ministry of Truth to rewrite old news, to reconstruct history so that it reflects well on the present regime. He's there to eliminate those elements of history that are uncomfortable or inconvenient. This erasure of history achieves nothing. It's not an honour to have a statue in your image or a building in your name a hundred years after your death. You're dead. It's no longer an honour, it's a *reminder*. It's a reminder of how we got to where we are. The good and the bad. Our history is being erased by students, some of them history students. All out of fear of causing offence. And yes, it's fucking Orwellian.

3

MARGARET THATCHER

THE MILK-SNATCHING GRANDMOTHER
OF DOWNING STREET

I don't wish to speak ill of the dead, but Margaret Thatcher was a fucking bitch. There's no getting around it.

When I was growing up, my mum would often use her as a threat. 'If you don't finish your greens,' she'd say, 'Margaret Thatcher will get you.' So effective was this threat that if I caught a glimpse of her on TV, I'd often piss myself. One of the reasons my parents voted Labour was that they couldn't afford to keep buying me pantyliners. I was thirteen at the time.

It's difficult to describe precisely how terrifying Margaret Thatcher actually was. Younger readers will no doubt think I'm exaggerating. But the truth is that although Thatcher died in 2013, her legacy lives on. Her ideals – known collectively as 'Thatcherism' – changed the political landscape forever.

Think you're too young to understand Thatcherism? Think again. Look around you. Whenever you see social inequality, homelessness, class division, that's Thatcherism. Try visiting any formerly industrial town in the north of England and talk to those older, angry generations. These are towns in which industries were sold off or closed down by Thatcher's government in the name of progress. We ended up with a generation of skilled workers who were left with no future job prospects and no way to provide for their families. We ended up with entire towns robbed of their identities, with homogenised high streets full of Wetherspoon's, Shoe Zones and, if you're lucky, the occasional Nando's. And these communities have never recovered. Consider the lack of opportunities for young, working-class people today. *This* is Thatcher's legacy.

Thatcherism was like a plague that infected all aspects of our society. She even managed to infect the Labour party who, under Tony Blair, willingly took on her obsession with the free market. In fact, when she was asked to name her greatest achievement she said: 'Tony Blair and New Labour. We forced our opponents to change their minds.' And the awful thing is that she's got a point.

Every prime minister since has tried in one way or another to emulate her style, with varying degrees of success. When Theresa May tries to imitate Thatcher, the results are often embarrassing.[1] Unlike Thatcher, May crumbles when she's under attack from the media. She's a vicar's daughter through and through, which means she's not naturally bullish and is out of her depth as prime minister. She'd be much happier being put in charge of a tombola at the church fete. Plus, Thatcher's hair was always immaculate, whereas Theresa May often looks as though she's just rolled out of bed.

The similarities are there, of course. They're both known for being stubborn negotiators, neither have particularly progressive policies when it comes to immigration or welfare, and neither have a pulse. For fuck's sake, they've even got the same initials, albeit in a different order.

Thatcher came from fairly humble origins, being the daughter of a grocer who was born in the small flat above a corner shop where there was no indoor heating or running water. This meant that she was able to connect with poor people later in life. In fact, she loved poor people so much that she spent most of her time in office enacting policies that generated as much poverty as possible. You may also recognise this approach in the more recent Conservative governments.

After a stint as Secretary of Education in 1970, Thatcher

---

[1] Theresa May was the prime minister when this went to print. One imagines by now it's Boris or some other posh, privileged turd.

was dubbed 'The Most Unpopular Woman in Britain' by *The Sun* newspaper, beating some pretty stiff competition from Mary Whitehouse and Myra Hindley. The reason Thatcher was so hated was that in an effort to cut public spending in education, she decided to end free milk at schools for primary school children. Calcium, after all, is overrated, and surely it's better to have a generation of brittle-boned kids rather than wealthy citizens who are taxed proportionately?

And so 'Thatcher the Milk Snatcher' was born.[2] It was a cheap nickname really, but the media love a good rhyme. Someone should have told her that if you have a name like that, it's probably best not to go snatching anything. You're only asking for trouble.[3]

Thatcher became leader of the Tories in 1975, having successfully challenged Ted Heath for the role (i.e., stabbed him in the back). She had all the necessary attributes: she was tough, she was unyielding, and she had apparently had her conscience surgically removed at birth, which for a Tory is always considered a major bonus.

---

[2] What 'Thatcher the Milk Snatcher' begun, Theresa May is now dutifully trying to finish. Not content with depriving young children of liquids, May has moved on to solids. During her election campaign in 2017 she pledged to abolish universal free hot lunches at schools. And her plan to replace them with free breakfasts turned out to be disingenuous; calculations revealed that she had budgeted for 7p per breakfast which, as Jeremy Corbyn pointed out, was the equivalent of a thimbleful of Rice Krispies. That's the Tory economic policy for you. We can afford the snap and the crackle, just not the pop.

[3] It's like when Virginia Bottomley went into government and then introduced her hugely unpopular health reforms. It was only a matter of time before the media worked out that 'Virginia Bottomley' is an anagram of 'I'm an evil Tory bigot'.

She was also a married mother of two, which meant that she could pretend to be a normal human being, rather than a harpy who had to keep her scaly wings hidden in a twinset. Thatcher married Denis in 1951 and gave birth to twins Mark and Carol two years later. Given their parentage, the twins were bound to grow up with their own problems. Mark turned out to be an international arms dealer, and Carol a reality TV star who was sacked from *The One Show* for referring to a professional tennis player as a 'golliwog'. Still, that's what happens when your mother craves the blood of the poor throughout her pregnancy.

When she eventually became prime minister in 1979, 'Thatcher the Milk Snatcher' was surpassed by a new moniker – 'The Iron Lady' – which actually started out as an insult from a Russian newspaper who were pissed off at her opposition to communism. In what was a very smart move by Thatcher, she reclaimed the term and wore it as a badge of honour.[4] Let's not forget that 'Tory' used to be a insult as well, until the conservatives embraced it as their own. I couldn't give a shit if they've embraced it or not. For me, 'Tory' will always be an insult, because it's the word you use to describe fucking Tories.

You'd think that Britain's first female prime minister would be a trailblazer for women's rights. But Thatcher didn't

---

[4] In the same way that Nigel Farage proudly refers to himself as 'The Great Cock Womble'.

much care for women. 'I don't like strident females,' she once said, evidently not realising that this was probably the most accurate description of herself. She was openly antagonistic to feminism and rarely promoted female colleagues. She even had elocution lessons so that she would speak with a lower, more masculine voice. Because apparently the more you sound like Brian Blessed, the more people will take you seriously.

The Thatcher years were characterised by mass unemployment, privatisation and rising inequality. And yet she still managed to win three consecutive general elections. The success of Thatcher is, if nothing else, concrete evidence that Great Britain is a nation of masochists and also an indication of quite how awful an opposition leader Neil Kinnock was.

Thatcher wasn't really interested in welfare, because obviously we live in a meritocracy, so if you're poor that must be a sign of laziness. With that rationale, there's really no point in offering handouts to those living on the breadline. They'd only go and spend it on wild luxuries like food and clothes and stuff like that.

Her disdain for the working classes came to a head in 1984 when she forced the closure of 21 coal mines, leading to a year-long miners' strike. In spite of pleas from struggling mining communities, Thatcher refused to compromise. And worst of all, refused to offer any support to those left struggling in the aftermath, instead characterising these desperate people as villains. By the end of the strike these communities were decimated, hundreds of working-class families were plunged into destitution, and the trade unions were fucked. What this proved was that Thatcher's approach to government was nothing short of tyrannical.

In spite of Thatcher's onslaught against the welfare state,[5] her contempt for the working classes,[6] her determination to sow division and resentment among the population,[7] it would be churlish of me not to admit her one legacy that we can all admire. Before she went into politics, Thatcher worked for some time as a food scientist, and it was while employed by J. Lyons and Co that she helped develop the Mr Whippy style of ice cream. So next time you're relaxing on the beach with a 99, spare a thought for the woman who made it all possible. Actually, don't. The idea of licking anything out whilst thinking of Margaret Thatcher is enough to make your cock fall off.

Thatcher was a capitalist, through and through. She instigated the 'Right to Buy' scheme, through which council houses could be bought from the government. The theory was that with more people owning their own homes, there would be greater prosperity.

---

[5] Sound familiar?

[6] Sound familiar?

[7] Sound familiar?

Bullshit. The reality was they were told to buy their own homes with money they didn't have, which resulted in crippling mortgage payments that they couldn't afford. Ex-council house tenants were now having their homes repossessed by the banks, meaning these people found themselves in need of social housing again. But, of course, there wasn't any left because the government had sold off all the council houses. Somebody really should have thought all this through.

It's fair to say that Thatcher saw poor people as an inconvenience. She wasn't a fan of the gays either. And if you were poor *and* gay... well, you may as well be euthanised for all the good you're going to bring to society.

As far as Thatcher was concerned, all gay people brought to society in the 1980s was AIDS. If it wasn't bad enough that the gays had given us Liberace, now they were trying to wipe us all out with their evil bum plague.

It's only fair to put this into some kind of perspective. In the eighties, it was quite normal and proper to think of gay people as degenerate sodomites. As late as 1990, *The Sun* was defending its use of the word 'poofter' in an editorial. 'Readers of *The Sun* know and speak and write words like poof and poofter. What is good enough for them is good enough for us.' This kind of editorial isn't imaginable these days, although the *Daily Mail* does still like to refer to Stephen Fry's 'husband' in inverted commas. It's just that kind of 'newspaper', I suppose.

Thatcher was concerned that gay people were determined to convert people to their cause, especially vulnerable children. As a solution, she brought in the now infamous Section 28 of the Local Government Act 1988, which prohibited the 'promotion' or the 'acceptability of homosexuality as a pretended family relationship'. Gay people, Thatcher reasoned, don't come from families. They're grown in laboratories on pieces of damp sponge.

For some reason Section 28 didn't work. Even though teachers were not allowed to acknowledge the existence of homosexuality, some children still grew up and fell in love with people of their own gender. This could either be because sexuality is an innate quality, rather than something learnt from political manifestos, or because the country had a prime minister who dressed and sounded like a shoddy drag act.

One of Thatcher's favourite phrases was 'there is no such thing as society'. Of course, if you don't believe that society exists, it's a lot easier to shit all over it and not worry about cleaning up the mess. Other phrases she liked include: 'the lady's not for turning', 'Nelson Mandela is a terrorist', and the immortal 'I fight on, I fight on to win' (uttered the day before she resigned her post having lost a Tory leadership contest).

There was also her bizarre announcement upon the birth

of her first grandchild. 'We have become a grandmother', she told the press, adopting the royal 'we' as though she were the Queen of England. When people are deluded enough to think of themselves as royalty, we tend to have them sectioned to an asylum. For some reason, this madwoman was allowed to carry on running the country.

The problem was that Thatcher always thought of herself as not just the head of parliament, but the head of state. She considered her obligatory trips to Balmoral to be a 'tedious waste of time' (which, let's face it, is probably the most accurate thing she ever said). In turn, the Queen reputedly referred to Thatcher as 'that woman', and mocked her accent as 'Royal Shakespeare received pronunciation from circa 1950'. Whatever the truth of their relationship, Thatcher's attitude towards the Queen certainly smacked of hubris. And if you don't know what hubris means, just look it up you lazy twat.

If relationships with the palace were a little strained, things weren't much better overseas. Thatcher had little genuine interest in foreign affairs, and during the course of her premiership managed to piss off every world leader (with the exception of Ronald Reagan, who clearly made her wet). She was only ever enthusiastic about international affairs when it helped her political career. If it weren't for the Falklands War she would never have emerged victorious in the general election of 1983. Just as her poll ratings were dropping, and people were starting to wake up to what a malicious prick she was, it all kicked off over in Argentina.

To be entirely fair, it was the fascistic Argentine junta that started the conflict, but Thatcher's response was hardly a milestone in diplomacy. By her orders, the *General Belgrano* (an Argentine navy light cruiser) was torpedoed and sunk, resulting in the deaths of 323 people. It was a controversial move, especially given that the ship was outside of the exclusion zone that had been set by the British forces. But hey, who cares about a few hundred human lives when you've got an election to win?

And indeed, all this went down pretty well with voters, because it allowed the ever-patriotic British to pretend for a moment that they were an important world power again. This in spite of the fact that Argentina was a nation known primarily for sheep farming and corned beef. It was hardly like going to war with Sparta.

Thatcher's popularity didn't last forever. After the wave of patriotism that the Falklands conflict generated, it was soon back to business as usual. After eleven years in office, Thatcher was finally ousted by her own party,[8] but the damage to the country had been done, and we're still nowhere near to a recovery. Thatcherism is alive and well in modern politics, and there's no sign of its influence

---

[8] Kenneth Baker (her home secretary who was portrayed as a slug on *Spitting Image*) started the coup by resigning over differences of opinion on Europe. It's always bloody Europe with these Tories.

abating. Little wonder, then, that in the week following Thatcher's death, the song 'Ding-Dong! The Witch is Dead' from *The Wizard of Oz* reached number 2 in the UK singles charts.

So to recap: Thatcher alienated female voters (otherwise known as half the electorate), stabbed her own party leader in the back in order to seize control, destroyed the trade unions, presided over a period of mass unemployment, instigated anti-gay legislation, and stole milk from young children. She was a self-interested, warmongering, anti-feminist megalomaniac who was determined to pursue economic policies that were guaranteed to increase the gap between rich and poor.

As with Theresa May, there is nothing progressive about being a female prime minister unless you are actually a progressive prime minister.[9]

Have I left anything out? Oh yes, her middle name was 'Hilda', which sounds a tiny bit like 'Hitler'…

But at least she gave us Mr Whippy.

---

[9] At Theresa May's first ever PMQs, she stood at the dispatch box and defended her party's feminist credentials. She pointed out that the Tories have produced the country's only two female prime ministers. It's difficult to argue with that one, really. But all it proves is that every thirty years or so the Conservatives will do one good thing for one specific woman.

4

ADOLF HITLER

VEGETARIAN

Donald Trump is not Adolf Hitler. Marie Le Pen is not Adolf Hitler. Nigel Farage is not Adolf Hitler. Sarah Palin is not Adolf Hitler. Jeremy Clarkson is not Adolf Hitler.

Adolf Hitler is Adolf Hitler. Well, he was, but the cunt's dead now.

All of this may seem pretty obvious, but it's worth pointing out because for so many on the left the word 'Hitler' has come to mean 'anyone I disagree with'. Other words that apparently have a similar definition are 'Nazi' and 'fascist', which these days can basically mean anybody who has reservations about immigration or voted Leave in the EU referendum.

Likewise, the 'far-right' used to mean racial supremacists, the elimination of political rivals through violence and intimidation to sustain a one-party state. It now means anyone who voted for Trump and anyone who hasn't caught up with which fashionable phrase is socially acceptable when describing black people.

Adolf Hitler was far-right. Tory voters and *Daily Telegraph* readers are, in the main, just right of centre. These distinctions are important. And in this chapter, I'll explain why.

I know what you're thinking. *Finally*, someone has the guts to put the boot into Hitler, to call him out for being such a tyrant. Let's be honest, everybody knows who Hitler was. Everybody knows about the Third Reich,[1] the Second World War and the Holocaust. Anything that can be said about Hitler has surely already been said. This is all true. So if you really want to know more about him, go and read a proper book.

And anyway, if I'm going to start including mass murderers in my list then why am I not discussing Fred and Rose West? What about Joseph Stalin and Mao Tse-tung, who were both responsible for more deaths than Hitler? I'm not saying it's a competition, but if it was they definitely would have won it.

---

[1] Are you seriously telling me you need a footnote to explain the Third Reich? How can you not know what the Third Reich is? You're a fucking idiot.

My interest in Hitler, for the purposes of this chapter, stems from the fact that his name has become a catch-all for anyone whose opinions do not comply with the morality police that lurk on social media, desperately trying to sniff out prejudice wherever they find it. Or, when they can't find it, pretending it's there anyway.

Now it goes without saying that I don't much like Donald Trump. The man is a corpulent, flatulent, bile-spewing narcissist whose self-esteem and bravado has an inverse relationship to his actual ability. But that doesn't make him the same as Hitler, and yet I have lost count of the number of times that people in the media have used their names in the same breath. Comparing Trump to Hitler is grossly unfair. For a start, Hitler was a good public speaker.[2]

Trump's attempts to curb immigration from Muslim-majority states may be a fucking ghastly and reprehensible thing to do, but it's not the same as rounding people up in concentration camps and murdering them *en masse* due to their race, religion, politics or sexuality. We have to be able to make these distinctions. If we don't, we risk undermining the sheer fucking brutal horror of what Hitler actually did, whilst simultaneously dismissing Trump's misdemeanours in far too simplistic terms. What

---

[2] Godwin's Law states: 'As an online discussion grows longer, the probability of a comparison involving Hitler approaches'. In doing so, a person invariably loses the argument whilst simultaneously believing they just won the argument. Remember the run-up to the EU referendum where everyone who was thinking of voting Leave was branded thick and racist by anyone intending to vote Remain? That strategy didn't work too well, did it? Same with Trump.

Trump is doing is different to what Hitler did. That's all I'm saying.

And it's not just Trump who gets branded like this. The LBC radio presenter James O'Brien recently read out an excerpt from Hitler's memoir *Mein Kampf*[3] and compared it with a speech given by Conservative Home Secretary Amber Rudd. Now, Amber Rudd may be a vacuous nonentity with a name that sounds like a skin complaint, but she's no Nazi. Or if she is, she definitely hasn't mentioned it to Theresa May.

Katie Hopkins[4] is another one who is routinely compared to Hitler. How many times have we read the phrase 'Katie Hopkins is a fascist!', screamed out into cyberspace, often in block capitals (because there's no better way of winning an argument than shouting it).

Katie Hopkins is not a fascist. She's a horse-faced careerist twat who thrives on attention. Every time somebody compares her to Hitler, or reports her to the police for 'hate crimes' because she's written something unpleasant about

---

[3] My German isn't great, but I think *Mein Kampf* translates as 'I'm a cunt'.

[4] Now I don't like *Apprentice* finalist Katie Hopkins. She has nothing of value to say. She literally doesn't know what she's talking about. Her writing about politics for the national press is as bizarre to me as if Kim Kardashian were to deliver a lecture on quantum theory. But she isn't breaking the law by having an opinion we don't like.

After Hopkins' infamous article about migrants in 2015, the *Independent* ran an article with the headline: 'Katie Hopkins has just written a piece so hateful that it might give Hitler pause – why was it published?' Now, I'm fully aware of the concept of hyperbole. I suspect I'm sometimes guilty of it myself. But whatever we might think of Hopkins (and I think quite a lot about her, much of it unpublishable) we have to accept that there is a difference between writing deliberately provocative articles for the *Daily Mail* and gassing Jews.

refugees or overweight people, they are ensuring that she'll keep on doing it. So well done for that.

Expanding the definition of 'fascist' to include the likes of Hopkins is an example of what is known as 'concept creep'. This is a typical strategy of the left, and it's one of the reasons why they need to get their fucking house in order. To give an example, a recent art exhibition in Canada was cancelled because the artist had been influenced by indigenous painters. According to one critic, because the artist was white her paintings were an act of 'cultural genocide'.[5]

This is what I mean by concept creep. Anyone who can't

---

[5] They call it 'cultural appropriation'. And it's become the favourite pastime of the loony elements of the left to root out and condemn. There have been cases in America of white students with dreadlocked hair being physically abused because wearing dreads if you're not black, it has suddenly been decided, is offensive to black people.

Which black people exactly? Trevor McDonald? June Sarpong? The black one out of S Club? You don't get to decide what black people are offended by. To do so is patronising... and racist.

By this logic most things we do are cultural appropriation in one form or another and need to be stamped out. Eating sushi, for example. Dancing to the Macarena. Shopping at IKEA. Spicing up your sex life by attempting the Kama Sutra.

Cultural appropriation is a good thing in most cases. Most cultures steal the best bits from other cultures. They always have. And sometimes they steal the Macarena. Cultural appropriation means opening yourself up to the world, not shutting it out. Because if you do that you realise where this logic ends? That's the end of art. The end of fiction. No writer can write about anything but their own experience. Every book will have to be a fucking autobiography, and we know how tedious they are. Segregated restaurants. Italian for Italians. Mexican for Mexicans. Is it cultural appropriation if I listen to Donna Summer? Should we have segregated concerts? Jay-Z and Lionel Richie for the blacks and fucking Adele and Coldplay for the whites, although Adele will no longer be able to perform or record any more because she is too highly influenced by MOBO and that clearly makes her a racist? Cultural appropriation is everything that is right with the world.

And so-called liberals need to 'check their privilege' before they accuse me of being racist for eating jerk chicken whilst listening to UB40.

tell the difference between the act of painting a picture and systematic mass murder on an industrial scale probably shouldn't be encouraged to discuss either subject. They should be encouraged to read a few more books, or just stay indoors where they won't embarrass themselves in front of the neighbours.

So let's clear this up. A 'Nazi' is not somebody who believes that nations should have secure border control or should keep immigration to a minimum. A 'Nazi' is not somebody who believes that diversity quotas are not necessarily a good thing. A 'Nazi' is not somebody who believes that the ideology of Islam has some questionable elements. A 'Nazi' is not somebody who thinks that everyone should be entitled to free speech, irrespective of how nasty their ideas might be. A 'Nazi' is not somebody who disagrees with the use of gender-neutral pronouns.

A 'Nazi' is somebody who believes in most or all of the following: the superiority of the Aryan race, the abolition of political opposition, an end to press freedom and individual free speech, territorial expansion by violent means, and the killing of communists, Jews and gay people. You'll note that the list doesn't include voting UKIP or watching repeats of *Top Gear* on Dave.

The word 'Nazi' actually has a very specific meaning. It's an abbreviation of '*Nationalsozialistische Deutsche Arbeiterpartei*' ('National Socialist German Workers

Party'), and since the German language is such a fucking mouthful they had to shorten it.

The misuse of the words 'Hitler', 'fascist' and 'Nazi' has violent consequences too. Because, believe it or not, the right hasn't got the monopoly on bigoted nutcases. Since Trump's election, we've seen the rise of a group who call themselves 'Antifa'. This is a militant body who engage in and promote the use of pre-emptive violence against those they deem to be fascists. Which basically means anyone they don't like. They call themselves 'Antifa' because they like to think of themselves as anti-fascist, but aren't educated enough to know how to spell the whole word.

These are the people you see on TV in black masks, smashing up university campuses if they have the gall to invite anybody who is right-wing, throwing rocks at police, and pepper-spraying Trump supporters. These are people who hate the concept of free speech, who genuinely believe that the best way to oppose fascists is… to behave like fascists. Well irony isn't everyone's strong point, is it?[6]

---

[6] I am aware in this chapter I have defended Katie Hopkins, cultural appropriation and UB40. If this chapter is messing with your mind, don't worry. David Cameron is up soon. That might be more your cup of tea.

5

RUPERT MURDOCH

The Lizard of Oz

Remember when newspapers[1] used to just inform you of what was going on in the world, instead of constantly trying to push a political agenda?

No, me neither. Most sections of the media abandoned the concept of impartiality decades ago. And that's thanks to the influence of one man. The money-grabbing, power-mad, turtle-headed[2] Antipodean who goes by the name of Rupert Murdoch.[3]

---

[1] The etymology of the word 'newspaper' is self-explanatory. A newspaper is news on paper. Hence, news-paper. Newspaper. The emphasis being on the news… you'd think.

[2] In both meanings of the word: (1) the head of a turtle, and (2) a turd emerging from an arsehole.

[3] Murdoch's first name is actually Keith, but you can't run a ruthless global corporation with a name like Keith. Nobody would take you seriously.

Murdoch is the founder of News Corporation Ltd., the many-headed beast that dominates the world's television, Internet, and news outlets.[4] For more than half a century he has been pursuing his goal of owning as much of the world's media as possible, and governments everywhere have allowed him to get away with it, especially when he provides them with plenty of favourable coverage (or perhaps that's just a coincidence).

Through his vast media ownership, Murdoch has created a wider trend towards sensationalism. That's why even the supposedly 'sophisticated' papers are more like tabloids than they used to be. It's dumbing-down on an international scale. Murdoch has given the whole world a very slow lobotomy without bothering with an anaesthetic.

He has been described by some as a 'self-made man', on the grounds that he managed to build up his business empire from nothing. If, that is, by 'nothing' you mean 'inheriting a massive fuck-off fortune from his already hugely successful father'.

In his early days, Murdoch established several newspapers in Australia, including the imaginatively titled *The Australian*. After pretty much taking over the media in Oz, he set his sights on the UK where he seized control of *The Sun* and the *News of the World*.

---

[4] Rupert Murdoch is at the front of a long line of media moguls including Robert Maxwell (who owned the Mirror Group and stole millions from his employees' pension funds, only to die when he 'fell off' his luxury yacht) and Elliot Carver (who attempted to start World War III in order to sell more papers, and died when James Bond planted his face into a big drilling machine).

The Sun is a good example of how Murdoch poisons everything. You're not going to believe this, but when it was launched in 1964 *The Sun* was an intellectual, left-leaning broadsheet that published serious articles on politics and current affairs. Murdoch bought the paper in 1969 and, visionary that he is, realised that what the public really wanted wasn't to be informed, but to perv at women's bare breasts. Rupert to the rescue! He immediately rebranded it as a cheap, sensationalist Tory wank rag full of ill-informed rabble-rousing and, most importantly, lots of tits.

Let me be clear. I'm not averse to the concept of a tabloid newspaper, an easy-read that is accessible and fun. And I'm definitely not averse to the occasional pair of tits.[5] But the problem is that Murdoch's papers and news channels are nakedly partisan. Look at Fox News, whose coverage of Donald Trump is fawningly sympathetic. Quite how anyone could have any sympathy for that creepy Dorito is beyond me, but they've somehow found a way.

Murdoch moved to the United States in 1974, where he immediately started buying up newspapers and magazines.[6] His technique is terrifyingly simple (if you're

---

[5] For the record, I believe that page 3 is an outdated and overtly misogynistic way of selling papers and I do not like it at all. And besides, who needs page 3 when you've got MammothMelons.com in your bookmarks?

[6] It's interesting that in the UK we have a tradition of our print media being partisan and our broadcast media being balanced. It has historically always been the opposite in the US, where they have a violently brash partisan broadcast media and a relatively balanced print media. Murdoch has seen to it that it's now a fucking free-for-all no matter what medium we're talking about.

a multi-billionaire). Buy up and control as many outlets as possible. That way the consumer has the illusion of choice; you don't have to read *The Sun*, you can read *The Times* instead. Problem is, you still get the same right-wing narrative in *The Times* as you do in *The Sun*, just with longer words. If numerous media outlets are all saying the same thing, it would appear that there is a consensus. If 75 per cent of newspapers say Jeremy Corbyn is an IRA-sympathising, Queen-hating waste of human skin, then it must be true. But not if those newspapers are owned by the same man.

In the eighties Murdoch went on a full-on spending spree. He began with *The Times*, then one of the most respected newspapers on the planet, now a thinly veiled tabloid.[7] He subsequently bought the *Boston Herald*, the *Chicago Sun-Times*, and Twentieth Century Fox as well as a major publishing outlet, Harper & Row (which later became HarperCollins).[8] He also sought to dominate

---

[7] It is in fact a tabloid: a tabloid is technically a newspaper that has its pages half the size of those of the average broadsheet. Of course, virtually all broadsheets have now reduced their size, possibly because you needed two seats on the train to read them. When *The Guardian* reduced its size, it couldn't bring itself to become a full tabloid, so they went halfway between tabloid and broadsheet. It's a little bit like their politics, not on the right, but not exactly on the left either. This half-sized format is known as the 'Berliner'. Trust *The Guardian* to go for the most pretentious option.

[8] I've been into the HarperCollins office. It's like if the Death Star had a publishing wing.

television by buying up lots of American TV channels, forming the juggernaut that is Fox Broadcasting.

You'd think the public's patience with this man would've run out years ago, but it wasn't until 2011 that the shit really hit the fan. It transpired that the *News of the World* had been illegally hacking the phones of numerous celebrities, and even sank so low as to hack the phone of murdered teenager Milly Dowler. It outraged the public to such an extent that, at the subsequent hearing,[9] a protester hit Murdoch with a custard pie. Yeah, that'll teach him!

For a man who is so good at PR, Murdoch somehow didn't anticipate that hacking the phones of dead children wouldn't go down well with the public. This is because, unlike Murdoch, most members of the public have a fully functioning human heart. Murdoch's only priorities are money and power. Even his wife is a status symbol. Why else would he marry Jerry Hall, a woman half his age and twice his height?

According to *Forbes*, Murdoch's net worth is over $12 billion. That's a personal fortune higher than the gross domestic product of many third-world countries. Let that sink in. We operate within a world where we are told that this level of inequality is not only deemed acceptable, but

---

[9] A lot of people (the Hacked Off lot) want stricter press regulations on the back of this scandal. I'm not a fan of that idea and I'm not sure it's necessary. What I am a fan of is journalists working within the law. If you hack someone's phone you should go to prison. You don't need stronger press regulations, you just need to enforce the present regulations and law to their full extent.

essential. And the people telling us this are the very same bastards who are at the top of the tree. So of course it's in their interests to sell us this bullshit.

At the time of writing, Murdoch is attempting a corporate takeover of Sky. There's a lot of legal wrangling going on but it'll happen in some shape or form. This would mean Murdoch would end up with total control of Sky News, in addition to all the other media outlets he already owns. The EU claimed they had no concerns about Murdoch expanding his empire in this way, whereas after the phone-hacking scandal UK lawmakers concluded that Murdoch is not a 'fit person to exercise the stewardship of a major international company'. This just goes to show that opinions of Murdoch vary depending on who you ask. Some think he's a power-mad fuckhead who needs to be stopped at all costs. Others think he's a power-mad fuckhead who should be given as much legislative support as possible so long as he'll help get them elected.

Murdoch will endorse any politician who will enable him to make more money; that's the bottom line. That's why he supported Margaret Thatcher, Tony Blair, Donald Trump, all of them passionate advocates of the free market.[10] Their policies make it easier for him to

---

[10] It's interesting that all three of these people have their own chapters in this book of political arseholery.

expand his empire, and in return, Murdoch gives them more and more approving coverage. It's a vicious circle of cuntery, and it fucking stinks.

The media shouldn't be cheapened like this. A free press is one of the cornerstones of democracy, because those in power need to be held accountable. The press should not be treated like a commodity to be bought and sold to the highest bidder. It shouldn't be cynically manipulated in order to make one media mogul as powerful as possible. It shouldn't be monopolised in order to advance a capitalist, right-wing political worldview that benefits only the very richest in society.

I'm sick of our politicians getting into bed with this vile man. It's a grotesque corporate orgy: presidents, prime ministers and CEOs, all scrabbling for a taste of Murdoch's withered old arsehole. With Jerry Hall somewhere in the middle.

6

KING HENRY VIII

THE MISOGYNISTIC GUTBUCKET
OF TUDOR ENGLAND

I'm crap at history. Too much reading. I dropped it at GCSE and did drama instead. This means I know fuck all about the crucial events that shaped our world, but I can improvise a short play about bullying.

However, when pitching this book I said it would be an exploration of politics through the ages, and the publishers are holding me to it. So I am contractually obliged to write a chapter that's got history in it, and I do happen to know a little bit about King Henry VIII, so here goes.

King Henry VIII was a syphilitic wife-murdering bearded whale who ruled England from 1509 to 1547. And when

I say rule, I mean it. Not like these modern royals. Even though this was after Magna Carta,[1] and parliament had been fully established, the King had ultimate control.

In a 2015 poll of 'Worst Monarchs in History' (pollsters have a lot of time on their hands), Henry VIII came out at the very top of the list. Given the behaviour of English monarchs over the centuries, this is quite a feat. If ever you need an argument against inbreeding, just look at the history of the British royal family. King John was a sexually aggressive sadist who used to starve his enemies to death. King Æthelred the Unready (silly name) massacred scores of Danish immigrants (silly man). And King Richard III allegedly butchered his nephews and then couldn't find his horse or something so went looking for it in a car park in Leicester where he remained for thousands of years.[2]

Arguably, Henry wasn't such a bad king at all. He was a Renaissance man[3] of formidable intelligence. He was a talented linguist,[4] a scholar[5] and theologian,[6] and

---

[1] Don't worry, I'm not going to start throwing Latin phrases at you like some sort of Etonian floppy-haired knob. But Magna Carta is important and you need to know this shit. It's the charter that was drawn up during the reign of King John in order to limit the powers of the Crown, and it underpins key values of our modern democracy.

[2] I told you my history was a bit hazy. But a contract's a contract.

[3] A clever dick who knows allsorts about allsorts.

[4] He could order a coffee in French and Italian.

[5] He could, like, read and write and shit.

[6] He thought about deep shit.

an accomplished musician.[7] His investment in education and the arts transformed Britain into the cultural and academic centre of the world. But none of this helps my argument, so I am choosing to ignore it.

Instead, let's start with looking at his habit of beheading wives, which is surely a flaw by anyone's standards. You've all heard the famous mnemonic: 'divorced, beheaded, died; divorced, beheaded, survived'. Here's a tip: if you have to come up with a special phrase to remember what happened to your wives, marriage is probably not for you.

What this tells us is that Henry was a shagger. He put it about. He wanted to shag and marry whomever he wanted, whenever he wanted. And only one man was standing in his way: God[8]. Or to be more precise God's PA, the pope.

Divorce was prohibited in Catholic England, so when Henry decided he wanted to leave his wife for Anne Boleyn, one of the ladies in waiting at court, he needed to get an annulment. The pope told him to go fuck himself (although he would have said it in Latin), and so Henry was left in a dilemma. He could carry on with his loveless marriage to Catherine of Aragon – who had so far failed to produce the male heir that Henry so desperately wanted – or he could establish the Church of England and then he could get divorced and slip a royal length to whomever he liked.

---

[7] He played saxophone in a pub jazz band.

[8] Or woman, depending which gender you prefer your imaginary deities to be.

In fact, the entire English Reformation[9] wouldn't have happened were it not for Henry's libido. When we think of the Church of England, we usually picture summer fetes with bunting, cream buns and sugary cups of tea, all presided over by a cordial buck-toothed vicar. Whereas the entire institution is the result of Henry VIII wanting to fuck one of the staff.[10]

So we've established that Henry was a philanderer,[11] a glutton[12] and a serial warmonger.[13] You might say we

---

[9] The English Reformation is basically when we moved from our church being Catholic and headed by the pope to what is now known as the Church of England, which is headed by the monarch. Which is why our Queen is still head of our church and state.

[10] According to some sources, Anne Boleyn had six fingers on one hand. Some historians have dismissed this on the grounds that it is unlikely that Henry would have been attracted to such a feature (body-shamers!). Actually, there are advantages to having a sixth finger. I'll leave it to your imagination.

Fair play to Anne Boleyn, though. Henry had been fucking her sister Mary for quite a while, even though Anne was the hotter one. When Henry tried it on with Anne, she refused, saying she'd only have relations within wedlock. By resisting the advances of a sex-pest, she altered the entire course of English history.

[11] For some reason, the Vatican is in possession of Henry's love letters to Anne Boleyn, in which he expresses his desire to 'kysse' her 'pritty duckys'. Which is Tudor-speak for 'Let me suck on your titties'.

[12] See 'Fat-shaming King Henry VIII' at the end of this chapter.

[13] He obsessively kept trying to conquer Scotland (but that was probably so he could get his hands on their shortbread and deep-fried haggis). And during his reign he was also continually at war with the French. In fact, Henry's wars depleted the royal coffers to the extent that by the end of it all the realm was bankrupt. To make matters worse, he was too fat to lead his soldiers into battle. To borrow one of Shakespeare's phrases, Henry was a real 'horse back-breaker'.

Did I actually just quote Shakespeare? What a wanker.

should be grateful that our modern royal family have none of these terrible qualities. But scratch the surface, and they do have one thing in common with their globulous ancestor. It's probably best summed up in one word: entitlement.

This, to me, is the problem with the idea of having a royal family at all. I'll be honest, I'm no monarchist. Why should I give a shit about Prince George, for example? I hate the twat. I had to stand outside that fucking hospital for four days reporting nothing while we all waited for him to be born. Why does he deserve all this attention, love, privilege, power and immense wealth just because he emerged from a royal vagina?

True, the royals these days aren't exactly like King Henry VIII. They're not cutting off people's heads or ransacking monasteries and I've got nothing against them as individuals (apart from that little bastard George). In fact, I feel rather sorry for them. It must be a dysfunctional existence, really, being forced to constantly open day centres and shake hands with poor people.[14]

The thing is, having a head of state who has inherited that title makes a mockery of democracy. Queen Elizabeth II is technically entitled to overrule parliament in a number of scenarios. And although this is never going to happen, the principle of the thing does matter. Besides,

---

[14] Mind you, all those servants, luxury accommodation, fine dining and millions of pounds at their disposal must be some kind of consolation.

Prince Charles isn't exactly known for his reticence when it comes to exerting his influence on political figures. It's the very thin end of a diamond-encrusted wedge.

Then there's the cost. We give them £35 million per year in taxpayers' money, and in return they expect us all to fawn over them. It's like a form of collective national Stockholm syndrome. We have literally fallen in love with our oppressors.

Think about it. We hand over large sums of money to these people, and then we go out and watch them spend it, and we wave flags. Under any other circumstance, wouldn't that classify as a mental illness?

It's just all a little embarrassing. Whenever any of these freeloading toffs decide they want to marry[15] their fucking

---

[15] Or die, of course. What about the fever pitch when Princess Diana died? If you're too young to remember (I fucking hate you) then just google it.

Now don't get me wrong here. I'm not one of these total cynics who doesn't appreciate the inherent tragedy of a premature death. I cried at her funeral. The bit when her brother's voice cracked as he said the word 'sister' in his eulogy. It was the moment I realised an actual person had died and not just a royal celebrity. And I thought about how I'd feel if my sister died and I cried. So there!

It felt pretty raw to all of us because Diana was the most photographed woman in the world. She dominated the media. Whether you were a royalist or a republican, you couldn't avoid her. We saw her every day whether we liked it or not. So, it was shocking when she was suddenly just gone. But I wonder if many confused shock with genuine grief.

In retrospect, we have to accept that the national response bordered on hysteria. Swathes of people, who could never have dreamed of having Diana's kind of privilege, descended on to Buckingham Palace to leave flowers and teddy bears that many could barely afford in commemoration of a woman they had never met. Everyone watched that funeral on the TV. We all bought into it. We all (not me) bought into the idea that Tony Blair's tribute was heartfelt. We all bought into the idea that Elton John's reworking of 'Candle in the Wind' was wonderful and appropriate and in no way trite. In reality it's actually quite ghastly, despite the fact that 30 million copies of it were sold worldwide.

The benefit of hindsight is a wonderful thing. It allows us to be a bit more ▶▶

cousin or something, it's us that has to pick up the fucking bill. I don't mind congratulating a married couple. And it's always nice to have a day off but, unless it's my own daughter that's getting married, I shouldn't have to pay for it. I've never met William and Kate. I don't care whether they get married, live in sin, or just occasionally bang each other in a Travelodge. It's none of my business.

What was especially cretinous about that particular royal splurge of taxpayers' money was this idea that Kate Middleton was somehow one of us, a real 'salt of the earth' type. What utter bollocks. She may technically be a 'commoner', but she comes from a wealthy family, is descended from aristocracy and, of course, was privately educated. Given that only seven per cent of this country has had that privilege, Kate is hardly representative of the 'common folk'.[16] One imagines her hen party didn't involve any inflatable willies and Lambrini slammers.

We paid for that wedding. The fucking taxpayers. And yet the majority of the UK population not only don't seem to mind, but they actually enjoy it! Has it never occurred to these people that there is something seriously fucked up about the whole situation? I can't imagine being a member

---

realistic and measured about the whole affair. Yes, it was a tragedy. But that didn't justify this unprecedented outpouring of grief. Why were we not in a state of bereavement for everyone else who died that year? Mother Teresa kicked the bucket a week later, and hardly anybody noticed.

[16] The media is an industry overwhelmingly dominated by the privately educated. As Owen Jones points out in his book *Chavs*, more than fifty per cent of the top hundred journalists share this educational background.

of the royal family and not thinking to myself, 'hang on, maybe this isn't really all that fair'.

Because this is *real* privilege. Not the 'straight white male privilege' we're always hearing about from the Liberal-Left, who have largely forgotten about the significance of class. Consider this. There is a family – as in, a small group of related people – who are funded to the tune of millions by the rest of us, who spend most of their lives drenched in opulence, who have the best healthcare available to modern science, and have every imaginable luxury at their disposal. And the head of that family is also our head of state. What the fuck is going on?

In a sense, I can forgive Henry VIII for his swaggering sense of entitlement. In his defence, he was living during the sixteenth century. Back then, they believed that the monarch was appointed by God. If you're raised to believe that an almighty being has placed you on the throne for the good of all mankind, it's bound to go to your head.

But Queen Elizabeth II is alive *today*. Right fucking now. In the twenty-first century. We have a crisis of homelessness in our country, and our government has just given the Queen a whopping £369 million to spruce up Buckingham Palace. This isn't just a loft conversion we're talking about.

And meanwhile homeless people in this country die, on average, at the age of 47. Elizabeth is almost twice that age and is showing no signs of slowing down. That's what money does for you.

I rest my fucking case.

THE GREY BOX

Fat-shaming Henry VIII

We should probably talk about the elephant in the room: King Henry VIII was morbidly obese. I know I'll be accused of 'fat-shaming' – or 'body-shaming', to use the more politically correct term – but in Henry's case I think it's totally appropriate. There's a difference between being a bit on the heavy side, and stuffing your face at every opportunity to the point where you're confined to your bed because you're too heavy to walk properly. And that's exactly what Henry did to himself. One of his advisors should have staged an intervention.

It's not fashionable to point out, but sometimes people get large because they're fucking greedy. According to historian Susanne Groom, a typical first course on one of Henry's 'fast days' was 'soup, herring, cod, lampreys, pike, salmon, whiting, haddock, plaice, bream, porpoise, seal, carp, trout, crabs, lobsters, custard, tart, fritters and fruit'.

That's a *first* course. On a *fast day*. So I don't want to hear any complaints about how poor Henry must've had a slow metabolism, or that he was suffering from some kind of hormonal imbalance.

He wasn't a victim of his hormones. He was a fat twat.

More to the point, Henry actually died of obesity-related illnesses. According to some reports, his weight resulted in his corpse 'leaking' when it was in his coffin, with stray dogs lapping up the residue. He might have avoided such an undignified end had he opted for a few Ryvitas from time to time.

7

DAVID CAMERON

A STORY OF PRIVILEGE,
ENTITLEMENT AND ARROGANCE

We need to talk about pigs.

A prime minister's legacy can often be judged in fairly simple terms by what they leave in their immediate aftermath. Often this means the prime minister that replaces them, whether it be by election or by the sword. In this case, David Cameron's successor was Theresa May, who soon came unstuck when she called a general election in order to gauge her level of support. Turns out she didn't have any.

Cameron's legacy includes two major misdemeanours. The first resulted in our impending exit from the EU. The second, though less important, is a rather wonderful thing. PIGGATE.

When it comes to political legacies, pigs rarely feature

in the discussion. Most politicians like to be remembered for their thankless years of public service and for making a valuable contribution to the general improvement of society. Few would rather their legacy be dominated by a sex scandal in which it was purported that they once fucked a pig. And yet this is precisely the position in which Cameron finds himself.

There's just one problem with the pigfucker story. It's bollocks. When you consider that the story came from Lord Michael Ashcroft, alarm bells start ringing. Ashcroft is a Tory peer who had donated £8 million to the party only to be passed over for a high-level job, and who then broke the story in the *Daily Mail*. So we know it's bullshit.

If we on the left are going to start crediting the *Daily Mail* as being a factual news source then we're going to have to start talking about how straight white men are the most oppressed minority in Britain. By virtue of this, it's safe to say that David Cameron is not actually a pigfucker.

I want it to be true. Of *course* I want him to have fucked a pig. We all do. But he didn't. And even if the story turned out to be true, Lord Ashcroft didn't actually say that Cameron fucked a pig. He said that Cameron placed his flaccid penis into a dead pig's mouth which isn't the same thing.

There's a photograph of me that exists somewhere, which was taken on my nineteenth birthday in a Wetherspoon's in Bridgwater. In it, my trousers are around my ankles and the end of my penis is dangling into a bag of Mini Cheddars. Obviously this photograph doesn't prove in any way that I have a sexual penchant for savoury pub snacks. It merely proves that I was a stupid drunk teenager.

Of course I know that a dead pig seems more severe than a bag of Mini Cheddars, but it could just have easily been a bag of pork scratchings. Which is worse in a way. Because that's not just a dead pig, that's a dead pig that's been ripped into tiny pieces, fried and salted. After that, slapping a cock on it isn't going to make much difference.

Um, where was I? Oh yes, David Cameron…

Well, let's begin with the coalition. In the 2012 election the Liberal Democrats did amazingly well because their leader Nick Clegg had appeared on the TV debates and, unlike his competitors, hadn't come across like a greasy salamander in a suit. Cameron didn't do quite as well and failed, therefore, to get enough support to win a majority. So, the Lib Dems and the Tories teamed up to form a coalition government. When you enter a coalition you obviously have to negotiate terms. You ask for things whilst giving other things away. You make demands and give concessions. It's like a marriage, but with even less sex.

For example, the Lib Dems wanted a referendum on changing the voting system. They achieved this by promising to abandon their pledge to abolish tuition fees. It must have seemed like a reasonable exchange at the time.

Their referendum was to change to the 'alternative voting system' which, for anyone who can be bothered to look at how the system actually works, is clearly a vastly fairer way of... well... voting. But when asked what they'd prefer, given the choice, the electorate went for... For fuck's sake. They can't even get a vote about a vote right!

Five years after the coalition came to power it was time for another election, and we were all expecting a similar result; both main parties were preparing for a potential coalition with the Lib Dems. That's why all of their manifestos were stuffed with policies that they would be happy to give away. Like a referendum on the UK's membership of the European Union, for example.

The Tories ended up winning an unexpected majority, so the feeling seemed to be 'let's get this fucking EU referendum over and done with as quickly as possible and then we get on with governing'. Well, I don't know about you, but I'm still waiting for that governing to begin. Since the day Cameron announced the referendum we have been in a perpetual state of political shit-holery: elections, referendums, leadership battles and brinksmanship. That's great for people like me and Andrew Neil because we need the overtime.[1] It's not so good if you're a normal human being who prefers to

---

[1] I need the overtime because of a messy divorce and Andrew Neil needs the overtime because of his penchant for fast cars, fast women and hair transplants.

watch *The One Show* and not have it hijacked by MPs trying to convince us all that they are human beings. When it comes to politicians, particularly Tory ones, I tend towards David Icke's assessment that they are from an alien race of malevolent lizards.

The Lib Dems were blamed for everything in that coalition. But under Nick Clegg the Lib Dems did a pretty good job of reining in the worst excesses of Cameron's government. If the Lib Dems hadn't have been there we would've had motorway privatisation, limited workers' rights, cuts to sustainable energy, weakening of the Equalities Act, cutting inheritance tax for millionaires and the abolition of the Human Rights Act. But because coalitions are all about compromise, the Lib Dems were forced into accepting a rise in tuition fees at universities.

And this is the thing that pissed off Lib Dem voters most of all? Come on. Never mind that Cameron was busy dismantling our public services. He wanted the Lib Dems to be the scapegoats, and the electorate fell for his ploy.

This explains the whole problem with democracy. It involves the general public, and the general public are fucking thick.[2] Rather than punishing the Tories, the voters punished the Lib Dems for reining in the Tories.

---

[2] I don't really mean this, of course. Or maybe I do. Depends on my mood, really.

In the 2015 general election, the Lib Dems went from fifty-seven to eight seats in what the party's leader Nick Clegg described as a 'cruel and punishing night'. But the voters were punishing the wrong party, weren't they? The stupid fuckers.

Anyway, with his new majority and with no Lib Dems left to object (as was supposed to happen), Cameron realised that he would have to finally settle the Europe question within his own party.

He should have been more careful. What fucked Thatcher? Europe. What split Major's government to the point where the gears of Westminster ground to a halt? Europe.

And it continues... Theresa May called the snap election in June 2017 for one reason only: Europe. She wanted to secure a stronger majority so that she wouldn't have to bother placating the Eurosceptics in her party. And, once again, because of Europe she got fucked![3]

Anyway, enough about Europe; let's get back to Piggate, because although it's not true, I still enjoy talking about it. Mostly because of the degree of humiliation that Cameron has had to endure as a result. It doesn't really matter whether it's true or not. What matters is that for a glorious period in our nation's history, the entire

---

[3] In the ass. Hard!

population were imagining their prime minister fucking a dead pig, and that's got to count for something. That's what is particularly interesting about Piggate; whilst we all know it's bullshit, we all also know that it seems oddly plausible. There's just something about Cameron that makes you think: 'Fucked a pig?... He stuck his cock in a pig and fucked it?... Yeah, I'll buy that.'

It says a lot about the man's character that we were all prepared to accept this rumour so readily and not dismiss it out of hand, as we might have done with Michael Howard for example. Actually, I wouldn't put it past him either.

In politics, rumours don't need to be true. It's like when Donald Trump was accused of hiring Russian prostitutes to piss on the hotel bed once occupied by Barack Obama and his wife. This clearly didn't happen – for one thing it involves a level of ingenuity that Trump completely lacks – but that doesn't stop us revelling in the story.

Perhaps it's got something to do with Cameron's insanely privileged upbringing. Cameron is a fifth cousin to the Queen, and was educated at Eton and then at Oxford University where he was a member of the elite Bullingdon Club. This exclusive all-male group has always attracted a certain type of student. Invariably, they come from the tweed blazered, upturned-collared, regatta-loving set who have triple-barrelled surnames and eat things like 'deconstructed cheesecake'. The Bullingdon Club are known for smashing up restaurants just for the fun of it, and then dismissively throwing money at the waiters to cover the damage.[4] They are also famous for their contemptible initiation ceremonies, which reportedly include burning £50 notes in front of beggars.[5]

In Ashcroft's biography of Cameron, an anonymous former member of the Bullingdon Club offers the following summary: 'What it basically involved was getting drunk and standing on restaurant tables shouting about "fucking plebs". It was all about despising poor people.'[6] So a bit like a Tory party conference, then.[7]

To be fair, it's not that Cameron despises the poor (like Thatcher did), he simply doesn't understand them. Having never struggled to survive financially, he lacks any concept of what it must be like to find somewhere affordable to live, or to provide food and clothing for your children. In other words, it wasn't so much his wealth that was his problem, it was his lack of imagination.

Let me give you an example. In one interview Cameron said: 'The papers keep writing that my wife comes from a very blue-blooded background, but she's actually very

---

[4] I'm not shitting you.

[5] I'm not shitting you.

[6] Seriously, I'm really not shitting you.

[7] At the 2016 Tory conference activities included a shooting range. That's right, you can even practise shooting grouse between seminars on how to fuck over the poor. They think of everything. In the conference brochure, there was an event listed called 'Solving Poverty the Conservative Way' where it was specified that gin and tonic would be served on arrival. That's what it actually said. 'Solving poverty the Conservative way'... with a gin and tonic! Makes me want to fucking puke.

unconventional…' Wait for it… 'She went to a day school.'
So Cameron thinks that if you don't go to a boarding
school you're 'unconventional'. That's fucking mental.
But that's the prism through which he sees the world.[8]

That's not to say Cameron didn't do his best to *pretend*
he knew what normal people like and care about. He
would sing along to Ed Sheeran in an attempt to appeal
to the 'yoof'. He'd support a football team and then
forget which football team he said he supported. He was
photographed with a husky, proving beyond doubt that
he cared about the environment. And let's not forget
his misjudged and frankly terrifying suggestion that we
should all go out at night and 'hug a hoody'. I live in the
east end of London, and believe me, if you're on the way
home from the pub and you encounter a group of young
men wearing hoodies, the last thing you should do is start
cuddling them. I would instead advise you to continue
walking but suddenly pretend that you're chewing gum
as if you don't give a fuck if they stab you or not. Works
like a charm!

By attempting to seem trendy, Cameron hoped to shore
up support among the hipster community. He pushed for
more liberal social policies such as anti-discrimination
laws and same-sex marriage. At the same time, he also

---

[8] This is why it was so absurd when Cameron came to power and immediately
branded the Tories 'the party of equality'. His successor Theresa May went a step
further, calling the Tories 'the party of social justice'. I don't know how these people
keep a straight face.

had to keep the Conservative grassroots voters on side, which involved being a complete twat on issues like welfare and support for refugees. This is why Cameron's brand of leadership often resembled a man suffering from a multiple personality disorder. He was servant to too many masters, all of whom had different agendas. Tory traditionalists don't much like the idea of equal rights for gay people, but they'll tolerate it so long as they can keep those pesky foreigners out. Especially the gay ones.

The more observant among you will have noticed that what I've said about Cameron, and how he was trying to appease those on both the right and the left, could apply just as readily to Tony Blair. In truth, when it came to their policies and ideas, there wasn't all that much between them. I remember watching them argue in PMQs and being reminded of Jorge Luis Borges's remark about the Falklands conflict: it was like two bald men fighting over a comb.

One way that you can tell if a politician has secured a legacy is if they end up with an '-ism'. There's Marxism, there's Thatcherism, there's Blairism, but 'Cameronism' hasn't caught on. There are two main reasons for this. Firstly, it sounds a bit shit. Secondly, Cameron was so inconsistent that it's difficult to pin down exactly what he stood for.

Unlike Thatcher, who didn't believe in society at all, Cameron wanted a 'Big Society'. This was really a cost-cutting exercise in which members of the public were invited to take over the running of welfare systems and public services so that the government didn't have to bother. It's a bit like the 'Clean for the Queen' campaign in 2016, in which the proles were invited to pick up litter to celebrate the Queen's ninetieth birthday.[9] Pick it up yourself, you lazy millionaire bint.

When considering Cameron's legacy, it is, of course, much fairer to judge the man not by his disgusting degree of wealth and privilege – or how many pigs he may or may not have penetrated – but instead on what he achieved during his time as leader of the Conservative party. As Cameron himself insisted, it's only fair to judge politicians by 'where they are going, not where they are from'.

Agreed. And what exactly was Cameron's destination? Well, by the time he left Downing Street, the country he left behind was one of rising national debt, rising inequality, and rising unemployment. Welfare systems were on their knees, the NHS was being privatised by stealth, and social mobility was a thing of the past. And, as a parting gift, Cameron left us with the almighty clusterfuck of Brexit. Good job, Dave.

I can forgive him most things. He wasn't a soulless

---

[9] In the end, hardly anybody took them up on the offer, but at least we got to see Michael Gove and Boris Johnson posing in those purple T-shirts with bin liners like a pair of total bellends.

gargoyle like Thatcher. He wasn't a gurning fraud like Blair. The reason he is here in this list of political cretiny[10] is because the man thought it appropriate to gamble away our country's future for his own self interest. Whether you're a Leaver or Remainer, that is the truth. He thought he could rectify the divisions in his party by settling the EU question once and for all, and assumed that the public would just vote the way he instructed them to. To my mind, this makes him one of the most reckless prime ministers of all time.

Perhaps the only good thing to come out of the whole Brexit debacle was that it proved to be the final nail in the coffin of Cameron's political career. Whatever you may think of the referendum result, it's some consolation to realise that every fear-mongering, doom-laden, fact-averse national debate has a big fat silver lining.[11] Wasn't it fucking great to see the back of that posh Etonian pig-fucking dickhead?

---

[10] Is 'cretiny' even a word? Doesn't matter. It's my fucking book. I make my own rules.

[11] On the morning after the EU referendum result, I was as shocked as everybody else. But as Cameron emerged from Number 10 following rumours of his imminent resignation, I sat at the end of my bed and said to myself, 'No matter what happens now, enjoy this moment'. And I did.

David Cameron

A Brexit Story

Once upon a time on a balmy sunny afternoon many years ago... Well, to be precise, I'm talking quite specifically about 23 June 2016. It had been a busy day. In fact, it had been a busy few months reporting on the run-up to our first referendum on our membership to the EU since we'd voted to enter it (technically the EEC at the time, back in 1975). And now the referendum was as good as over. The result was a forgone conclusion and

I had taken the next day off as I'd been pulling fourteen-hour days for the last fortnight and we all knew that as soon as the results were announced that it'd be back to business as usual.

So after work, before going back home to vote, the few of us who weren't working that night went to the pub and had a few. Before I knew it, it was 9:15pm. I was going to have to hurry if I was going to get to my local polling station in time. I've never missed the chance to vote in a national election, and I wasn't about to start now.

How did I intend to vote? I'd gone with instinct, really, and that was to vote Remain, even though my instinct is usually to do the exact opposite of what David Cameron says.

I entered the polling station in good spirits with minutes to spare, a little merry and confident in my conviction that, despite a few reservations, remaining in the EU was the only sensible decision to make. And anyway, I knew it was the right choice because everyone on my Facebook feed had been saying the same for months. Facebook was telling me that only a racist or a mentally challenged person would even consider voting Leave in the referendum, so it must be true. This was going to be easy, and if I was quick I'd make it back to the pub for last orders.

I pulled the curtain behind me in the booth, and held the pencil tentatively over the ballot paper. Then something happened. I became light-headed and unstable on my feet. I entered a trance-like state and a voice began to speak to me. I was becoming confused and disorientated. Who was it that was speaking to me?

Was it my conscience? Was it God? Was it the first signs of early onset-dementia? Or was it the six pints of Strongbow and whisky chasers? Either way, for some reason the voice I heard was unmistakably that of William Shatner.

Don't be alarmed. As a lifelong *Star Trek* fan, I often experience such visitations when I've had a few too many. Whether it's Leonard Nimoy urging me not to drunk-text my ex-wife, or George Takei materialising in All Bar One and reminding me to catch the last night bus home, I've just got used to it.

But this time, in the voting booth, marked the first time I'd been visited by William Shatner.

Captain Kirk himself. Time slowed. It was like one of those moments when your entire life flashes before your eyes. For example, if you're about to crash your car into a wall, or your future wife is walking towards you down the aisle looking like an Edwardian prostitute-cum-paper-lampshade.[12]

'Hey, Jonathan. You look confused,' Shatner said in his trademark breathless staccato tones. 'Of course you're confused. Everybody's confused. Because the only thing the media is talking about is who's gonna win and who's gonna lose. But something's missing! Information! How can you possibly make a decision unless you're properly informed?

'It's a tough choice to make. The EU is all about trade, the free market. Helping faceless corporations to thrive often at the expense of the poor. But the economic benefits are hard to deny. There are three million jobs in your country that depend on trade with the EU.'

The voice grew louder. 'Three! Million! Jobs!' it repeated dramatically. 'What happens to them if you leave? What happens if you restrict freedom

---

[12] I guarantee I was the first person that day to think 'I give it six months!'

of movement? What do you do about labour shortages? But if you sustain immigration at its present level, what happens to public services? Will the NHS be able to cope?'

And then Shatner appeared, resplendent in his Starfleet uniform. He looked me straight in the eye and continued.

'The real problem is nobody wants to admit that they don't know what'll happen if you leave. No country has ever tried it before.

'The Remainers say you should stay in to reform the EU. But history tells us that's not going to happen. You left-wingers have always been traditionally anti-EU and now we're in this weird situation where the only people who are making the traditional left-wing case are right-wing political jokers like Boris Johnson and Nigel Farage. And because everyone thinks UKIP are a bunch of racists, old-school lefties like you, Jonathan, are scared of being pro-Brexit by association.'

Shatner's arms flailed around as he began to talk of fear. 'This whole debate, if you can call it a debate, has been about causing fear!' he cried. And every time he uttered the word 'fear' he would pause dramatically, his eyes wild with excitement.

'Nicola Sturgeon says that Brexit will trigger another Scottish referendum. *Fear.* Nigel Farage says England will be swamped with immigrants. *Fear.* Labour's Keir Starmer says that staying in protects the country against terrorist attacks. *Fear.* Boris Johnson actually wrote an article with the headline "Don't be taken in by Project Fear – staying in the EU is the risky choice". Fear, or fear. Would you like some fear with your fear? The debate has been terrifying.'

Shatner paused. I swayed around the booth dizzy with confusion, my mouth filling with saliva.

'This referendum has exposed everything that is wrong with politics. Johnson said Hitler would have voted Remain, but Cameron says Brexit could trigger World War Three. If that were true, why would he ever give the Great British Public the option of voting for something that could potentially destroy the planet?

'Cameron also claims that ISIS are pro-Brexit. I always thought ISIS wanted the wholesale destruction of Western civilisation. But no! Like Captain Birdseye, they're more interested in the UK's fishing quotas. Yet again, another national political debate has descended into farce.'

Shatner's voice reached fever pitch. 'The left has *completely* abandoned its principles to support a body whose main purpose is to help massive corporations. And the right has made it all about personality over politics, which is a contradiction in terms when it involves a Tory.

'This is the choice you face, Jonathan,' Shatner exclaimed, his eyes penetrating my soul. 'Vote Leave and you're supporting Boris Johnson or Michael Gove. Vote Remain and you're supporting David Cameron.

'Johnson or Cameron. What a choice! You're caught between the devil and the deep blue twat!'

Shatner then started singing the theme tune to *T. J. Hooker* and slowly began to get undressed, at which point I vomited over my ballot paper and passed out.

Even now, a year or so later, I can't quite get my head around what happened in that voting booth. By the time I came to, it was three minutes past ten and it was too late to cast my ballot. But I still can't work out how I would have voted had I been sober.

William Shatner had given me no clear answers, and now Brexit is actually happening we still don't really know what it actually means. Theresa May, of course, has always insisted that Brexit means Brexit. Well, that clears that up then.

But what does it *mean*?

Back in January 2017 she gave a speech in which she said she was going to trigger Article 50, and confirmed that the goal was a 'hard Brexit'. That's what the debate has been all about ever since. Is it going to be a hard Brexit or a soft Brexit? Theresa May called it a 'clean Brexit' but let's be under no illusion: Theresa May likes it hard. Or, as the *Guardian* put it, 'a rock hard Brexit'. What are they going to come up with next? A gangbang Brexit? A bukakke Brexit?

Maybe I'm being facetious. I know that Brexit isn't black and white. I know that because according to Theresa May it's red, white and fucking blue. What the fuck does *that* mean? May clarified the remark by explaining that a 'red, white and blue Brexit' means a 'British Brexit'. No fucking shit. I was wondering what the 'Br' in Brexit meant, you stupid cow.

What does Brexit fucking mean?

The problem is no one knows what it fucking means. No one ever knew what it meant. We were never supposed to vote for Brexit. No one thought we'd vote for Brexit. Even people that voted for Brexit didn't think we'd vote for Brexit. And its all down to David Cameron, who assumed a vote about Brexit wouldn't mean Brexit but in the end it meant *his* exit and in a speech about Brexit to explain Brexit, May confirmed that Brexit means Brexit. And not just any old Brexit but 'a rock-hard-clean-red-white-blue British Brexit'. So that's nice and clear then.

From the very start the level of debate was appalling from both sides of the argument. Both sides have to take responsibility for this. There weren't any facts. It was all about who could say the most alarmist thing and get away with it. Fuck me, you even had Bob Geldof chasing fishermen down the Thames on boats. That's not reasonable political debate, that's like a dream you have when you've drunk too much Strongbow. One involving William Shatner, perhaps.

8

HARRY S. TRUMAN

EVERY MUSHROOM CLOUD HAS
A BRIGHT ORANGE LINING

Look at his little face. Looks like quite a friendly chap, doesn't he? A bit like the Werther's Original granddad, but not so creepy.

How could someone who looks like that possibly be on

this list of political and historical arseholes? What could he have done that's so bad? Truman was a Democrat, and vice-president to FDR, one of the greatest presidents in history.[1] He was a reluctant commander-in-chief and he was the man credited with winning the Second World War – the deadliest war this planet has ever seen. Doesn't sound too bad, does he?

However, Harry S. Truman has the dubious honour of being the only human in history to order the use of a nuclear weapon in combat. Twice, in fact.[2]

First he bombed Hiroshima, killing 70,000 civilians instantly. Then, one week later, he exploded a bomb over Nagasaki, leading to the deaths of a further 80,000. It is estimated that the collateral damage over time was the loss of 250,000 lives.

What a cunt.

Even if he'd not dropped two nukes, Harry S. Truman could still have easily ended up on this list of arseholes through the ages. For one thing, the 'S' in his name doesn't even stand for anything. What a pretentious prick.

---

[1] Franklin Delano Roosevelt or FDR (only the good ones are known by just their initials). The one in the wheelchair. Probably the nearest to a socialist the White House has ever seen. Author of the New Deal... 'The only thing we have to fear is fear itself'... That one.

[2] At time of writing there's quite a dramatic standoff going on between Trump and North Korea. So it's quite possible that by the time this is published half the planet will have been wiped out.

It is now an accepted part of historical narrative that dropping those nukes was a necessary evil that saved more lives than it cost by making Japan shit its pants and run for the hills. If you know anything about Japanese soldiers in the Second World War you'll know this is bullshit. These are soldiers who were willing to engage in kamikaze suicide missions, for fuck's sake.[3] So I just don't buy that they all downed tools simply because the US had started to flatten cities in minutes rather than days.

Arguably, the war was already drawing to a close. In fact, weeks before the first bomb dropped, Japan had tentatively made inroads as to how they might 'honourably surrender' (i.e., you win, but the Emperor stays!). Honour is everything in their culture, so to surrender outright was unthinkable. But if they could find a way to surrender and keep their head of state then the war could be stopped without further bloodshed. But why bother with diplomacy when you've got a brand-new weapon that you need to try out? This was all one big test. A test with tragic human consequences.

There's a sense in which Truman saw himself as a godlike figure, raining fire and brimstone down on the heads of his enemies. He wrote in his diary that the

---

[3] The Japanese were undertaking suicide missions years before al-Qaeda thought of it. Like with the electronics industry, they're always one step ahead. They saw death in combat whilst protecting the emperor as the highest honour. They treated prisoners of war with utter contempt because to them death was infinitely more honourable than being captured and staying alive. To them, POWs were the lowest of the low and that, rightly or wrongly (i.e., wrongly), is why they treated POWs so badly.

bombs would cause 'the fire destruction prophesied in the Euphrates Valley Era, after Noah and his fabulous Ark'. If that isn't the ravings of a madman, I don't know what is.

But this isn't all about the nukes. Truman was instrumental in the creation of the state of Israel. Trust me, I'm not fucking going there.[4] But we can all agree that it hasn't quite worked out as everyone hoped. Can we? Or can't we? Excuse me while I tiptoe gingerly out of this minefield...

Truman also got America involved in the Korean War, a pointless conflict that resulted in the deaths of around 30,000 US soldiers. But it did result in eleven seasons of the sitcom *M*A*S*H*... So it's a case of swings and roundabouts when it comes to this particular conflict.

And there was one other war that Truman was instrumental in starting. The Cold War.

It sounds a bit like a snowball fight or something, but in fact it was a power struggle between the USA and 'the West' on one side, and the USSR and 'the East' on the other. It centred around their two competing ideologies: capitalism and communism.

One of the problems was that Truman was ill-equipped to deal with the fallout of the Second World War. He didn't have the intellect of his predecessor Roosevelt, or much of an understanding of foreign affairs or the importance of diplomacy. It was ridiculous. It'd be like making Postman

---

[4] The subject, not the country. I hear there are some lovely beaches in Tel Aviv.

Pat the White House Chief of Staff. Or making Donald Trump the president. Mental.

Almost immediately on taking office, Truman declared privately that the moment the war was over, Russia could quite frankly go fuck itself. This was in spite of the fact that the Soviets had formed an alliance with the Americans in order to defeat the Nazis. I'm not suggesting for a moment that Russia was a paragon of virtue, but a deal's a deal, right? Right?

In dropping the bomb and reneging on promises made to their Russian allies, Truman laid the groundwork for the Cold War.[5] It was a 'war' in name only, in which not a single shot was fired. Doesn't sound too bad, does it? Just sounds like an extended edition of *Question Time*.

Of course, this is arguably better than the alternative, which is to say nuclear Armageddon.[6] But to suggest that there were no victims of the Cold War would clearly be fucking stupid. In case you're wondering, the estimated death toll of the Cold War is around 7 million. I have no idea how this is calculated. And I can't be bothered to do the research.

The Cold War went on from the end of the Second World War until the fall of the Soviet Union in 1991. But if no one was actually fighting, what the hell was going

---

[5] And let's be honest, there was a lot of heat before the war went cold: 17 million deaths in the First World War, and around 50 million in the Second World War.

[6] As Armageddons go, that's one of the worst.

on? It was more about propaganda and espionage, about an arms race and escalating tension, about the possibility of war rather than war itself.

The Cold War was based on the sobering fact that both sides had the capacity to wipe out the other, and themselves for that matter, several times over. So it was a stand-off, like a big international staring competition with an understanding known as 'mutually assured destruction'. The rule was that if anyone were to let off a single nuke, for any reason, then everyone else is obliged to follow suit. Mutually assured destruction, otherwise known (wholly appropriately) as MAD!

The moment those nukes were dropped on Japan one of two outcomes became almost instantly inevitable: either nuclear Armageddon, or an arms race within a perpetual state of Cold War with the threat of nuclear Armageddon ever present. This is Truman's legacy.

As I said before, what a cunt.

THE GREY BOX

*From the Industrial Revolution to
postmodernism*

Let's talk about the Industrial Revolution for a moment.

We're talking toddlers getting their hands trapped in spinning jennies, locomotive steam engines, bridges and shit. Boats made out of iron that still float. A fucking flying machine. A fucking machine that fucking flies? Fuck off! An actual flying machine? No, but how does it... a fucking machine that flies? In the air? Fuck off!

But despite all the advances in manufacture and transport, the industrial age only really started picking up steam once one particular set of circumstances visited all four corners of this planet. War!

They say that necessity is the mother of invention. And if necessity is the mother, then war is probably the father, albeit one that tends to get drunk down the pub every night and smash up the kitchen in an attempt to cook a late-night omelette.

Lots of things were invented to deal with the unique circumstances of war: wristwatches, tea-bags, tampons, and of course guns. War has propelled the world's scientists into making great advances in medicine and transport, not to mention giving us the Call of Duty franchise.

Nobody would deny the importance of these inventions. But if there was one thing that we'd probably all like to see un-invented, it would most likely be the nuclear bomb. Once you've split that atom, you can't just Sellotape it back together again.

There comes a point where a weapon of such horror and indiscriminate destruction is invented that there is quite frankly nowhere else to go. There's no going back. Our civilisation has reached a point where all life on earth could conceivably be obliterated as a result of the technology we created. The invention of the nuclear weapon was, in other words, an epoch-changing moment.

This might seem a little tenuous. But when I look at the effects of postmodernism, I can't help but see a connection. At the core of postmodernism is the idea that we are merely products of the society and time in which we live. That there is no grand plan or any such things as universal beauty and truth. That's why we now look at an unmade bed in an art gallery and see in it the kind of value that our predecessors might have seen in the Sistine Chapel. Because we don't know what anything means any more. We don't understand the value of value.

This is why when I see Andy Warhol's pictures of tins of soup, I think of Hiroshima. Now I know that soup is not on a par with an atomic weapon. Soup is a simple and tasty source of nutrition, essential to all recovering from a nasty cold or a recent divorce. An atomic weapon is something else entirely.

But now that we live in a world in which the possibility of total annihilation is conceivable, it's very easy for scepticism to take over, to believe that nothing really matters. Everything is as priceless / worthless as anything else because we're all doomed anyway.

So, in a way, Truman was the father of post-modernism. Sort of.

Like I said, tenuous. But it bumped up the fucking word count a bit, didn't it?

9

SIMON COWELL

Britain's Got
(very little) Talent

The McDonald's hamburger is the most eaten hamburger on the planet.

The Fast and Furious films are collectively the highest grossing movie franchise of all time.

More people alive on the planet have read *Fifty Shades of Grey* than have read *A Tale of Two Cities*.[1]

The most read newspaper in the UK is *The Sun*.[2]

Mrs Brown's Boys was recently voted the best sitcom of the twenty-first century.[3]

One Direction are the biggest band on the planet right now.

---

[1] Probably.

[2] The second most read is the *Daily Mail*. Make of that what you will.

[3] Beating the likes of *The Thick of It*, *Peep Show* and *The Office*! I'm not being a snob. I'm not. *Mrs Brown's Boys* is, admittedly, not my cup of tea (although I quite like it when they pretend to crack up). But best sitcom of the last seventeen years? Come on.

The human race never ceases to amaze in its capacity to consume vast amounts of diarrhetic shit through its mouth, its eyes, its ears and, in the case of reading *The Sun*, through its soul.

So, who is to blame for this cultural dumbing-down on an almost global scale that has infected all aspects of our lives,[4] including what we watch, what we read, who we vote for, what we eat and which awful auto-tuned songs we listen to on smart phones that cost a month's wages to buy but are only built to last for no more than a year or so?

Who is to blame? Capitalism? Consumerism? The Internet? Our failing education system? No. Simon Cowell is to blame.[5]

I like Simon Cowell. Nice chap. He has always been pleasant on the few occasions that I have met him. He actually once gave me a lift in his gorgeous Bentley. (What a car!) I was a bit star-struck to be honest. And that never happens. He was an absolute gent, and we chatted quite easily for the time I was alone with him in his car, about everything from our differing perspectives on fatherhood (he has a nanny and custody, I have neither) to the implications of Brexit. Brexit is unlikely to have much of an impact on Cowell's wealth, but might

---

[4] I know in the Rupert Murdoch chapter I blamed Murdoch for this very thing. But that was then. This is now.

[5] Look, I'm not seriously suggesting that all the world's woes are Simon Cowell's fault, but for the purposes for this essay, I am. And he actually is to blame for One Direction.

mean that *Britain's Got Talent* will have to restrict its search for a star to the British Isles which, whilst fulfilling its remit more accurately, could be problematic. Let's face it, if *Britain's Got Talent* has proved one thing, it's that it hasn't.

I found that we had a lot in common too. Like him, I also enjoy pointing out people's faults.[6] So from the outset I'd just like to say that I respect the man deeply and would love an opportunity to work with him in the future.

That said, *Britain's Got Talent* is fucking shit, isn't it? So is *Pop Idol* and *The X Factor* and all of them. They're all shit. They are the TV equivalent of RateMyPoo.com.[7]

The world we live in appears to be in a state of intellectual decline. You just have to watch the news. It's no longer there to inform and to disseminate fact, it's there to regurgitate opinions from the ill-informed twitterati.

---

[6] I think we really clicked, and if our schedules were different I think we could have become firm friends and, who knows, maybe even colleagues. I was thinking maybe a new primetime show with current affairs and political analyses, interspersed with various pop acts competing in some way. We could call it *The Pie Factor*. It could do wonders for my career.

[7] RateMyPoo.com exists. Its premise is simple. People take a picture of their shit, upload it to the internet where people are then encouraged to rate the poo from one to ten. Disgusting, isn't it? And yet I have spent many a bored afternoon in the office rating other people's shit. As such it is the perfect metaphor for much of Cowell's output.

It's there to shout over and goad politicians to the point where they no longer want to say anything at all for fear of being torn to shreds. It's there to analyse inaccurate polls and sensationalise the mundane, and mainly, when the shit hits the fan, it's there to turn itself into a 24 hour rolling grief porn channel.

And yet not so long ago it was a different story. The TV news was admittedly dull and prosaic. Yes, there was spin and human-interest stories, but its main focus was on providing facts. When I started out in news broadcasting, things had started to change. 9/11 had heralded the coming of age for rolling news. Soon after, the news became about filling the airwaves with news stories around the clock. So they had to keep it interesting. They started filling the airwaves with ridiculous computer graphics, rolling tickertape that says nothing, and everything was suddenly 'Breaking News!' Whether it be a major terrorist incident or Eamonn Holmes getting a new fridge.

The news became a thing to entertain rather than inform. It became about punditry rather than analysis. So much so that we are left in a position where, in all aspects of society, we no longer see any distinction between opinion and fact. They have equal value. So when Simon Cowell says you're a good singer it means you must be a good singer, even though all other evidence suggests otherwise.

As such the news's main aim is to gather viewers and hold on to them. It's there to make money. And in some respects, that's okay. People like to make money. It's why most of us bother going to work each day. But aren't there some things that are more important? Is anything sacred enough to be protected from the worst excesses of a capitalist consumerist society? There is music as art and then there is the music industry. There is education for education's sake and then there is Tory education policy.[8] There's the NHS and then there is Bupa. There's *The Andrew Marr Show* and then there's *Good Morning Britain* with Piers 'I'm a smug-faced butter sculpture' Morgan.

I'm not saying that fluffy entertainment doesn't have its place. Not all art has to be high art. Not all music has to be Beethoven or Bowie. I'm as partial to a bit of white middle-class easy listening rock/pop (Keane) as anyone else. And I like shit television. I enjoy *Gypsy Wedding* as much as the next man. And I never found Clarkson-era *Top Gear* anything but inoffensive light entertainment for lads and dads. Crap telly is fine. It's a way to switch your brain off for a while.

---

[8] Everything is a commodity these days, including your education. Gone is the idea of education for education's sake. (What's the point of doing a Master's in history? It's not going to earn you a better salary. But history is fucking amazing and fascinating and can help you contextualise the world in which we now live.)

When you have an ex-Education Secretary (Michael Gove) coming out and saying that those who don't benefit from a university education shouldn't have to pay for it, you know you're in trouble. To be honest, if Michael Gove can find me one person in our country that hasn't been seen by a doctor, or who hasn't ever been to a school, or who has ever crossed a bridge without it collapsing, or has been in any building that has ever been designed and built, or used the Internet, then I'd consider not making them pay for universities.

But I'm convinced that the television we consume is making us all thicker. I know exam results get better and better, and world literacy is on the rise, but I have one small but indisputable piece of evidence to support my theory. *Bullseye*.

Bullseye was a Saturday night quiz show in the eighties based around darts. You can catch it these days on Challenge TV. I don't wish to appear snobby, but there really is no way around it: *Bullseye* was entertainment for the plebs. It was for people who have tattoos[9] and call their main evening meal 'tea'. The contestants were generally a bit greasy, had regional accents (still a fairly bold move back then) and the host was a working men's club comic.

Seriously, just compare the questions on *Bullseye* to any modern-day quiz show. *Bullseye* was for thick darts players and their unattractive wives, and they're answering questions about classical Greek culture. Correctly! They're answering questions about the music of Gustav Mahler. They're finishing quotations by Keats. It simply wouldn't happen now. Just thirty years later and your average question these days is: 'For £10,000, according to *Chat* magazine, which ex *Celebrity Big Brother* housemate's fake tits recently exploded whilst on a Ryanair flight to Magaluf?'

---

[9] Proper old-skool tattoos of anchors on the arm or hearts on your chest. Before they became trendy and everyone started having them, all up their necks or all over their entire leg. Always with a shit beard. And a short back and sides with a floppy bit on top. And what's with those fucking hoops in people's ears that make their earlobe all loose like a low hanging vulva? What is wrong with some people? You look awful!

In much the same way as Truman dropping the bomb irreversibly changed the world, there is surely a point of no return for a culture that applauds 'the middle of the road', that celebrates the 'not too bad'. The fact that a dog has won *Britain's Got Talent* (twice!) suggests that this cultural event horizon is almost upon us.

Just take a look at who is in the White House. The highest office on the planet is occupied by a reality TV show host cum glorified estate agent. When did mediocrity of such mammoth proportions become the benchmark? When did it ever occur to anyone that a man with no charisma, negotiating skills or political acumen, a man with the writing, reading and speaking skills of a pissed slug, was suitable for high office?

When it comes to the White House we don't have to look back very far to understand the conditions by which a Trump victory was made possible, or perhaps even inevitable. When you look at the Gore/Bush election of 2000, the Team Bush strategy was to paint their man as the folksy, plain-spoken, no-nonsense candidate. A guy to catch a game and eat a hotdog with, which is shorthand for 'not an intellectual'. So to win they created a narrative whereby being an intellectual was a bad thing. Gore was made to look like a stuffy elitist over-educated snob, and he lost because of it. They successfully dumbed down the presidency. On purpose. That was their election strategy.

What is wrong with wanting our leaders to be educated?

Surely it's better if they're smarter than the rest of us? But the US electorate clearly see it differently. When did being qualified, experienced, adept, articulate and the best person for the job become a disadvantage?

It's a waste of talent and a wasted opportunity. Elections should be about watching two smart sets of people with opposing views debate. We, in turn, are informed by that debate and then participate in the democracy via the voting booth, basing our choice on whose case was better argued. And yet these days we always get distracted from the discussion. Serious intelligent debate is abandoned in favour of mudslinging and soundbites and catchphrases. We always end up talking about something stupid and insignificant, like bacon sandwiches, or 'mugwumps'. And Cowell's entertainment industry is cut from exactly the same cloth.

We have a long history of celebrating mediocrity,[10] but Cowell turned it into a global multi-billion-pound business. He spreads cultural slurry on an industrial scale, shit-spraying us into submission until we actually believe that a dog jumping through a hoop to the strains of The Village People is decent entertainment.

These 'talent' contests also buy into our blossoming victim culture where we judge talent not in its own terms

---

[10] Shit talent shows, for example, aren't a new thing. *Britain's Got Talent* and *The X Factor* et al. owe a large debt to *Opportunity Knocks*, which is responsible for giving us the likes of Freddie Starr, Bobby Crush, Darren Day, Bonnie Langford, Su Pollard, Roy 'Chubby' Brown, Little and Large, Pam Ayres and, as if to ensure there was no confusion as to the quality of these acts, a band called Middle of the Road.

but against how shit your life is.[11] It's no good just to be an amazing juggler, you have to be an amazing juggler with AIDS whose cat recently got run over.

For example, Susan Boyle is not an amazing singer.[12] She's not bad. She has the sort of voice that would get the solos in the local church choir. But the reason she did so well is because she is considered unattractive and is clearly a bit weird in the head. And as we all know, unattractive people who are a bit weird in the head aren't supposed to have any talent at all. Especially when they're Scottish.

Another example is Rik Waller, a morbidly obese contestant who reached the final ten in the first series of *Pop Idol*. He did well not because his voice was amazing, but because he wasn't totally fucking shit whilst also being totally fucking fat.[13]

And let's not forget the singing itself. You know that particular *X Factor* style of singing that's all breathless and airy and sounds like your throat is made up of a toy car, some dirt and a twig? All those insincere gestures that no one ever uses in real life, like using your hand to write in the air with an invisible pen? None of which can hide the fact that your top notes are weak and your

---

[11] See the grey box at the end of the chapter. Although if you're a fan of the victim-centred brand of fourth-wave feminism, then maybe don't bother.

[12] *Britain's Got Talent* runner-up, 2009.

[13] I am not 'fat-shaming' here. The guy later went on *Celebrity Fit* (fat) *Club*, so he knows he's fat.

bottom notes sound like a fart reverberating round a toilet bowl.

The nearest we get to The Beatles these days are four or five sexually ambiguous boy-clones with underdeveloped larynxes, who think that wearing white suits and dramatically standing up from their stools in unison every time the key changes will disguise the fact that they have no discernible talent whatsoever.

It's an homogenised version of talent, where one act is pretty much indistinguishable from the next. The reason being that taking risks doesn't guarantee money. The best way to ensure commercial success is to please as many people as possible. But in my view, if no one hates what you do then you're doing it wrong. It becomes the equivalent of a McDonald's hamburger. As already stated, it's the most consumed burger on the planet, but is it the best? For most it's merely the least offensive burger, even though it has next to no nutritional value and sits in your stomach, slowly fermenting into one almighty deadly guff that takes you by surprise thirty-six hours later during an important meeting.

Let's be honest: the best part of any of these talent shows is near the start of the series where all the country's mediocrities queue up to get laughed at and scorned by very, very rich people. We've always loved a freak show, which is why I occasionally have a walk around Iceland, just for a laugh. Cowell is merely tapping into that very human instinct and has turned it into a multi-million-pound empire.

He is the face of an industry in which the homogenised, the mediocre, the stupid, the inarticulate, the uneducated, the 'easy-read', the fastest food, the saddest story, the emotionally unstable and the chronically untalented are revered and celebrated. An industry that feeds a world where the acquisition of fame supersedes any desire to hone a craft. Where narcissism rules. Where being personally offended (often a by-word these days for disagreeing with an opinion) is a crime on par with actual physical or sexual abuse. Where opinion must be respected more than fact. Where the 'fair to middling' are encouraged to delude themselves that they are the best of the best and that their opinion actually counts for something.

It's a world where every high street looks the same. A world in which you baulked at spending just over a tenner on this very book, but don't bat an eyelid when Starbucks charge you the best part of a fiver for what is essentially a pint of warm milk in a paper bucket. A world where our head of state is one of the richest women in the world and is adored, whilst people are sleeping on the streets a minute's walk from the palace, who are totally ignored.

A world where watching privileged, attractive yet ultimately vacuous people on a sunny island trying to fuck each other is considered entertainment. Where watching some twat from *Emmerdale* eating a crocodile's uncooked anal gland is a ratings winner. Where Ann Widdecombe makes it into the top TV moments of the year by prancing around a dancefloor like an injured gorilla in a tutu.

This is what the TV channels think you want. And the thing is, they're not wrong! You fucking lap this shit up willingly, and Simon Cowell has made millions out of ramming it down your throats.[14] He's like a feeder, stuffing us with 'entertainment' that neither enriches nor actually entertains. He gets off on watching you consume this shit. He masturbates at the thought of an entire nation giving itself a slow, self-induced lobotomy of the soul and he then mops up the jizz with the dollar bills you provide every time you phone in to vote for one of these talentless, out-of-tune amoebas. Simon Cowell isn't to blame for everything that is wrong with the world, he is merely the poster boy for it. A god-like creature in a cynical world where our art, our media, our humanity and our soul is trampled over in favour of a quick buck and a double page spread in *Hello!* magazine.

That said, he's a thoroughly decent bloke. And, if you're reading this, Simon, please bear me in mind for any future projects that you're working on. I've got a few ideas, actually... so um... you know, call me.

---

[14] Just in case there was any doubt as to quite how fucking shit some of Simon Cowell's output has been, here are a few of his worst misdemeanours. He is responsible for the novelty records of acts such as Zig and Zag (the Irish puppets from *The Big Breakfast*), *Power Rangers* (a bunch of teenage superheroes jumping around in spandex), the *Teletubbies* (a sort of sitcom for toddlers with an LSD habit) and the *World Wrestling Foundation* (now World Wrestling Entertainment, Inc., which boasts alumni including Hulk Hogan, The Undertaker and Donald Trump). Cowell is also responsible for the music career of Robson & Jerome, and the song 'So Macho' by Sinitta.

THE GREY BOX

A Culture of Offence

Victim culture and offence culture is rife these days, especially within left-wing politics. This is one of my biggest bugbears with the left. We've created a culture in which your opinion, your worth, sometimes even your job prospects are measured in relation to your perceived victimhood or privilege. It's called identity politics. And it is everything that is wrong with the Guardianista left. It's a narcissistic idea by which those who feel personally offended can demand that the world must change to suit their own particular outlook.

Just because you're offended doesn't mean you're right!

In the case of feminism, for example, the culture of offence and victimhood can actually be quite regressive. Do you remember that advert on the tube for Protein World? It had a big picture of a skinny woman wearing a yellow bikini, and in big letters the poster asked 'are you beach body ready?'

It caused outrage! There was a petition and everything. And *Stylist* magazine said that the advert was 'attacking women by promoting an unrealistic body image'. And in the editorial, it said that the advert used 'threatening block capitals'. That's right. Women are apparently so weak, so fragile, that even the sight of a bold font is likely to reduce them to to quivering wrecks. How fucking patronising can you get?

I'm not having a go at political correctness. It was my generation that pushed for it, because being polite to people is a good idea. It's about having an agreed way of behaving towards people in public spaces and in the workplace. But the idea has recently mutated into a competition to see who can be the most offended, the most victimised. And it simply doesn't achieve anything.

The cry of 'that's offensive!' has become a substitute for argument, a way to avoid listening to an alternative viewpoint. For example, to suggest that everyone who voted to leave the EU is a bigot is in itself the very definition of bigotry.

Another example is the left's favourite method of shooting down unfashionable opinions. They call it 'privilege'. Whether it be male privilege, white privilege, straight privilege. And the holy grail is 'straight white male privilege'. As a straight white male myself, I am aware that I am on very thin ice in attacking the phrase. But because I think it's fucking bullshit, I'm going to do it anyway.

There is a very strict hierarchy within identity politics, with straight white men at the very bottom of the pile. It is easy to see why if you look back at history. Many of us really were/are a right bunch of bastards. But we're in a position now where straight white male privilege applies no matter if you're a millionaire or living on the streets addicted to crack. Real privilege is, of course, about money. But it's far easier to make these tokenistic gestures than genuinely changing society for the better. I am often being 'called out' for being a straight white male (as if that's a great to surprise to me) and as such my opinions on certain subjects are deemed less valid.

This is not to deny anyone's lived experience. Of course there will be those who experience forms of prejudice that I never will. But ultimately, I am a human being who is capable of empathy and insight. My life experiences are as unique as anybody else's, and nobody should be making assumptions about my perceived 'privilege'.

It seems bizarre to me that anyone would call themselves a liberal or a progressive and yet label people in these terms. If anyone ever tells you to 'check your privilege', they are in effect negating their need to debate. It's a trick! They disagree with your viewpoint and so seek to silence you on the basis of your supposed privilege. It's utter, utter bullshit and it achieves absolutely nothing. It says everything about certain lefties that they appear to be obsessed with diversity, just so long as it isn't diversity of opinion.

By all means argue that my point of view is flawed. Feel free to disagree with me for getting my facts wrong, for being rude or patronising (see 'mansplaining' in the Glossary) but don't ever dismiss my argument or make assumptions or judgements about me based on my gender, my sexuality, or the colour of my skin! It is regressive bigotry hidden behind a thin veil of moral and intellectual superiority and it fucking stinks. Bad ideas are only defeated through debate and not by silencing those with whom you disagree.

There. Rant over.

10

DONALD J. TRUMP

(INSERT INSULT HERE)-IN-CHIEF.

Well, no great surprises here. I've saved the best for last.

At the time of writing, Putin and Trump have just met for the first time, the US has dropped out of the Paris climate agreement, the press secretary Sean Spicer has resigned, the chief White House strategist Steve Bannon has been fired, and Trump just decided over Twitter to ban transgender people from the military. Nearer to home, Theresa May lost an election a few weeks back, but at this moment in time she is still prime minister.

Remember all that? Well, that's where I'm at.

You, dear reader, are ahead of me in time. As you read this, Trump may have already been impeached and removed from office. He may have just won his second election. He may have just handed the keys of the White House to his daughter Ivanka.[1] Trump's head may well be carved onto the side of Mount Rushmore with a gift shop up his left nostril. He may even be long dead. But never forgotten. Because whatever happens, Donald Trump was once the president of the most powerful nation in the Earth's history. And that's never going away.

Has there ever been a comparable world leader? The only one in living memory that springs to mind is Russian President Boris Yeltsin. His presidency ended on 31 December 1999, and by that point he was no longer just a functioning alcoholic (which was hardly a secret anyway), he was a fully fledged drunk. He was ill, and it was plain for all to see. He was frequently seen in public and on television not just drunk, but properly fucking shit-faced. Pissed right up! It was clear to everyone that he was unfit for the job.

Trump is not a drunk. Or even a functioning alcoholic. He's not a drinker at all, apparently, but he is demonstrably a low-functioning sociopath with some serious personality disorders, and his unfitness for the office is just as clear to many today as it was with Yeltsin.

Of course, not all would agree with this assessment. If you are reading this and you voted for Trump, I would like to point out that whilst I do not agree with your decision,

---

[1] I've already put £100 on that one. Imagine in either 2020 or 2024 Ivanka Trump vs Michelle Obama. I might start taking better care of myself from now on because I want to be around to see that.

I do understand some of the reasons for it. I'm not going to start calling you thick or misogynistic or bigoted. I'll save that for the person you voted for.

If you voted for Trump I have to assume it was a considered act. Let us also assume, for the sake of argument, that many or most of those voters are happy with him as president. If that is the case, then that's roughly 12,465,000 people who, at time of writing, aren't completely baffled by President Donald Trump. The rest of us, however, continue on a daily basis to be utterly stunned and perplexed by the man's political ineptitude, his lack of diplomacy that appears to run through him at an atomic level and, of course, the colour of his skin.[2] The world changed the day Trump got elected and it's hard for most of us to think of many positives.

So what follows is not so much a chapter as a dossier that, I hope, will in some way explain three things. How did this happen? Why did this happen? And what's going on with his hair?

---

[2] Ed: That could be seen as racist.
Pie: Yes it could. By a complete cretin.
Ed: Okay, but it definitely counts as body-shaming.
Pie: Couldn't give a shit. It stays.

PART ONE
Chancer-in-Chief

(Or, How Trump Won)

There's nothing new about celebrities going into politics. Especially in America.[3]

Arnold Schwarzenegger was an Austrian body builder who became famous for pretending to be a robot, then subsequently became governor of California. Ronald Reagan was a crap matinee idol star who later became a crap president. With Alzheimer's. You can imagine the scene, can't you? 'Remind me again: what does this red button do?'

But how did this present shit-show occur? How did Trump do it? How did a reality TV star become the most powerful man on the planet?

It's worth pointing out that it could have been worse. Because frontrunner and bookies' favourite Ted Cruz is a right-wing zealot nut job and he would have taken the US back to the dark ages. If you think Trump's bad, he looks positively progressive when stood next to Ted Cruz, who is quite frankly a fucking maniac. He just wasn't making as much noise about it.

---

[3] When it happens in the UK it tends not to be quite so glamorous and a bit more downmarket. For example, *The One Show* (*Blue Peter* for adults) regular Gyles Brandreth was a Tory MP for a while, and daytime TV twat Robert Kilroy-Silk was an MEP for UKIP (in the early years). Although we also had Oscar-winning actress Glenda Jackson who was a Labour MP for years and was always there to add a touch of class in a slightly unhinged kind of way.

Trump, however, was loud! He was brash. And quite camp as well. Like a big pantomime dame without the dress or the make-up. Without the dress, anyway.

The biggest mistake the Republicans made was thinking Trump couldn't win the nomination. And everyone else made the same mistake too. The moment the Democrats thought they had it in the bag was the moment Clinton's fate was sealed.

Trump is attractive to the electorate for good reason. He's rich! When you're that rich no one owns you. An independently wealthy billionaire in charge could in theory be a great thing for America, because a billionaire is less constrained by having to please lobbyists and donors. As such, Trump's presidency could have been an extraordinary opportunity for change. He could have been great for the environment because he isn't in the pocket of the oil industry. He could have been great for healthcare because he isn't in the pocket of pharmaceutical companies. And whether this be true or not, it was at least a logical conclusion for the electorate to reach.[4] He represented the total opposite of Clinton, who was in everyone's pockets and had been for a long time. Once again, however, it's not that simple because this is Donald Trump: America's answer to a question nobody asked.

---

[4] The reality is that Trump's accession to the White House represents a wholesale corporate takeover of politics in America. The secretary of state is ex-oil. A guy from Boeing now runs the defence department, the White House is riddled with ex-Goldman Sachs bods. Trump even tried putting an investment banker in charge of White House communications. He lasted just under 10 days.

A man who hates Muslims, wants to build big walls around Mexicans and who thinks Obama faked his birth certificate because... well, Obama just looks like a foreigner, doesn't he? It's strange, because if we're going by skin colour, I don't think Donald Trump even qualifies as human, let alone American.

But who voted for Trump? Well, a lot of people did. But I believe that it was those who struggle the most that tipped the balance. If you are poor, unemployed, living in a trailer park with no prospects and you find yourself in a voting booth, for that second you are just as powerful as the richest person in the country. And you know what you're going to put your cross next to? Change. That guy in the voting booth wants change because he literally has got nothing to lose. And Clinton didn't represent change. She represented a neoliberal, corporate-sponsored status quo. She represented the political establishment.

The Democrats relied on the old adage 'if it ain't broke, don't fix it'. Well, it's been broken for a long time, and people chose the only tool available for the job. The biggest tool of them all: Donald John Trump.

Many people say it was a protest vote. I'm sorry, but if you want to protest, then go and fucking protest. Grab a sign, get some bongos, strap yourself to the front door of Goldman Sachs, whatever you need to do. But don't vote for a nut job. This is one of the most precarious times for international relations in human history. You shouldn't jeopardise the stability of the planet just to piss off snowflake liberals like me.

PART TWO
Toddler-in-Chief

Recently my son Conrad[5] got into trouble at school for calling his friend Tristram[6] a 'fuck monkey'. I can't think where he's picked up that kind of language.

I sat down with him and explained that you mustn't use bad language and you certainly shouldn't go around calling people names. I know this is rich coming from me but you've got to tell them something, haven't you? Otherwise they'd run riot. His defence was 'Tristram started it', which is probably what I would have said at his age. Although I like to think I'd have come up with something more imaginative than 'fuck monkey'. So I gave him a light bollocking and, as ever, he folded his arms and refused to speak to me. Just like his fucking mother.

The reason I mention this is that when Donald Trump was questioned about why he called American talkshow

---

[5] I know, it's a dreadful name. My (ex) wife chose it because the name runs in her family. When I pointed out that colon cancer runs in mine, and you wouldn't wish that on your firstborn, she didn't look happy and we had a big argument. I lost the argument. So Conrad it is.

[6] And you thought Conrad was bad. Some of the other kids in the class have it even worse. You can't move for Tarquins and Jolyons. But it's a good school. And by 'good' I mean that all the other parents are wankers.

host Rosie O'Donnell a 'fat pig', his defence was exactly the same as my son's. 'She started it!'

He has done similar to many others on countless occasions. Meryl Streep slags him off, so he says she's hugely overrated. CNN criticise him and suddenly they're 'fake news'. It's clear that these things are actually upsetting him. He's desperate for attention but only if it's the right kind.

Let's think about that for a moment. The leader of the free world is using the exact same tactics as a little boy who thinks he's going to have his iPad taken away from him.[7] My son behaves this way because my son is four years old. And he isn't a major political figure. And, let's face it, judging from his appalling handwriting and his inability to grasp even rudimentary grammar, he's never going to be.

Donald Trump, on the other hand, is a man whose job it is to forge relations with international leaders, who deals with very delicate and sensitive diplomatic issues on a daily basis. And here he is calling a woman a 'fat pig' because she made fun of him. She started it!

If he is so easily antagonised by talkshow hosts, actors and newsreaders, then just imagine what happens when world leaders criticise him. We all saw how he treated German Chancellor Angela Merkel when they first met at the White House. He actually feigned deafness rather

---

[7] Who decided iPads were suitable gifts for primary school kids? They're fucking expensive. Who gives an iPad to a child? (Answer: my wife's new husband.) It's a disgrace. They should be outdoors climbing trees, not gazing at a bunch of pixels on a screen...It keeps them quiet though, doesn't it?

than acknowledge her existence or shake her hand. It was quite, quite demented, and exposed his crippling lack of tact or diplomacy. He then went on to claim that he and Merkel had got on brilliantly, despite the fact we'd just all witnessed that this was palpably not the case.

Trump's lack of diplomacy is in fact the strongest case for his unfitness for office. Diplomacy is quite simply an agreed set of rules and appropriate behaviours within which people from different cultures and countries, with different opinions and ideologies, can discuss their shared goals and, more often than not, argue about their differences without resorting to shouting, mud-slinging, spitting or hurling faeces in the process.

Another word for diplomacy is political correctness. Or politeness. On an everyday level it's simply an agreed way of behaving in the workplace and in public spaces. But on a geopolitical level diplomacy is, quite frankly, all that keeps us from blowing each other up. Most of the time. Trump has demonstrated on numerous occasions that he lacks any diplomatic acumen whatsoever. And although it can often seem petty to point out his social *faux pas*, his inarticulacy, his bizarre awful handshakes or creepy flirting with certain heads of states' spouses, and his basic rejection of many or all diplomatic norms, this behaviour can often have serious global consequences.

Like all small children my son lies quite a lot. Silly things. And he is never ever to blame for anything. He's also started wetting the bed again, but at least he's not hiring Russian prostitutes to do it for him.

One of Conrad's most epic meltdowns was when more people went to Tristram's birthday party than his. Sound familiar? Donald Trump claims that 1.5 million people attended his inauguration. That's more than three times the official estimate. So, who are we supposed to believe? The facts as presented by qualified and experienced news broadcasters? Or the little chattering phantom clowns that dance about in Donald Trump's head, whispering to him their 'alternative facts'? Or maybe just use your eyes to look at pictures of the crowds. Do that and Trump's alternative facts are immediately exposed for what they are: lies. Which he covers up with *more* lies.

After we had that discussion about the 'fuck monkey', I banned Conrad from playing with his iPad, and he freaked out. He ran out to the back garden and kicked the cat flap until it snapped off it's hinges. And when I caught him, he denied it and just said, 'It wasn't me!'

This was in spite of the fact that I saw him do it and he saw me see him do it. And that's exactly what Trump would have done. First, he would have denied kicking the cat flap. And then he would have questioned the very concept of cat flaps. Then he'd say that neither cats nor flaps are real and are the invention of a corrupt media with a partisan agenda. Then he'd probably make a witty remark about pussy flaps.

Just look at what happened when he mocked disabled reporter Serge Kovaleski. When he was criticised for it he simply said it didn't happen. Even though we all saw it happen. It's right there on YouTube for anyone to see. Trump then claimed that he couldn't have been impersonating Kovaleski because he'd never met him and didn't know what he looked like. But again, the thing about facts is that they can be verified. You can actually check them out. Trump had met this reporter on numerous occasions and was even interviewed by him in his own office!

Trump's instinct is always to hit back. To lash out when he doesn't get his own way. To cry and scream and stamp his feet. These are the characteristics of a six-year-old child and one thing we do know about six-year-olds is that they have no social skills and like pressing big red shiny buttons. Yet the American people saw fit to elect this child to the highest office in the land.

Trump is, quite simply, a little boy in a man's body. A boy who has always got his way, who has never been punished when he's done something wrong. A spoiled, toxic little man-child whose body just grew up quicker than his brain and his fingers. A shrill, petulant, bloody-minded, foot-stamping, hand-wringing cry-baby who surrounds himself with sycophants as if he's King Henry VIII. A whining, attention-seeking, insecure, paranoid, self-centred, slobbering insult to nature who coasts callously through life, oblivious to his own good fortune, giving nothing but taking everything. He's a graceless, charmless, talentless fuck monkey of a man.

Fuck monkey! I like it! That's my boy!

PART THREE
Tweeter-in-Chief

To the rest of the world the US is a TV show which we all enjoy watching. Problem is they're now on season 45 and it's all gone a bit weird. It's all just flashbacks and dream sequences these days. They've jumped the shark. They've nuked the fridge. They've done a liquid shit on the White House lawn.[8]

This means that reporting on this administration can, at times, seem almost impossible. How do you report the news from a White House that is arguably from another dimension?

Most journalists these days start their day in exactly the same way that I do. I get up, and before even switching on the news I go for a dump and get on Twitter to see what

---

[8] 'Jumped the shark' is a phrase used when a long-running TV show runs out of ideas. It comes from when the US sitcom *Happy Days* had an episode when 'The Fonz' attempted to water ski over some unconvincing stock footage of a shark. 'Nuked the fridge' is another version of the same thing derived from the film *Indiana Jones and the Kingdom of the Shitty CGI* where Harrison Ford survives a nuclear blast by hiding in a fridge. Some British versions could include 'crashing the tram' in *Coronation Street*, 'reanimating Dirty Den' in *EastEnders*, and 'impregnating Sue the panda' in *Sooty & Co*. I've always suspected the real father was Bungle.

explosive controversy the president has concocted today to shift focus from the fact that he's a bit shit at his job and he's yet to pass any effective legislature.

For journalists, Trump's tweets are the news equivalent of a stun grenade. We used to turn up to work looking for an exciting angle to report the world's news. These days at around 5:30am POTUS gets up, takes his dump (which, by the looks of him, can be an explosive controversy in itself) and he chucks a tweet-shaped stun grenade at us all.

BANG!

The entire world's media is blinded by the complete absurdity and inarticulacy of what he has just written. We spend most of the day trying to decipher what he actually means. His Twitter handle is actually '@realDonaldTrump'. It's almost as though he has to remind people that he isn't a parody.

Let me say for the record that I fucking love Twitter. For those who don't know (the over-45s or those who have actual jobs or meaningful relationships for example) Twitter is an online forum for the exchange of ideas. At any moment you can post a comment regarding absolutely anything, so long as it's no longer than 140 characters. This can be read by anyone at all, so it's a public domain. It's a way for people to connect, express ideas, and share and read articles from the world's press, no matter where they live. It's truly democratic in that sense, as it means everyone can be a part of the conversation.

Sure, there are pros and cons. Twitter contains the

whole range of the world's opinions and as such it can spread bad ideas as well as good ones.

Donald Trump has been on Twitter for years, way before he embarked on his political 'career'. Back then, he was an entrepreneur and reality TV star, so it was all about keeping his profile going. That's why he would tweet things like the following:

> *Robert Pattinson should not take back Kristen Stewart. She cheated on him like a dog & will do it again--just watch. He can do much better!*
>
> – 17 October 2012

If only Hillary Clinton had been more on the pulse of celebrity gossip, she might have stood a chance in the election.[9]

The trouble is, now that he's president, Trump's reasons for using Twitter haven't changed. Before he was elected, he said that he if he won he wouldn't tweet any more because it's 'not presidential'. Like everything else he's ever said, we should have taken that statement with a pinch of anthrax.

Trump now says that it may not be presidential to tweet the way he does, but it is 'MODERN DAY PRESIDENTIAL' (1 July 2017). What's he's effectively doing is fusing his two careers. For him, the presidency is no different than

---

[9] That said, Clinton did appear on the same stage as Beyoncé and Jay-Z during her campaign. It's strange how this didn't swing the vote her way. It's almost as though the political expertise of hip-hop and R&B stars counts for nothing.

starring in another series of *The Apprentice*. It just adds to his profile, further inflating his ego (if such a thing is possible). This isn't a real presidency, it's a hybrid of politics and reality TV.

Sometimes his tweets make this all too explicit. Take the following assessment of the former governor of California:

> *Arnold Schwarzenegger isn't voluntarily leaving the Apprentice, he was fired by his bad (pathetic) ratings, not by me. Sad end to great show*
> – 4 March 2017

Why is a sitting president making the kind of bitchy comments you'd expect from Perez Hilton? And why should he care anyway? After all, as he later tweeted:

> *The W.H. is functioning perfectly, focused on HealthCare, Tax Cuts/Reform & many other things. I have very little time for watching T.V.*
> – 12 July 2017

You're not *meant* to be watching TV! Do you know why? Because you're the commander-in-chief. You've got the world's largest superpower to run. Remember that?

More worrying is that Trump clearly doesn't consult any of his advisors before tweeting out what often appear to be major policy announcements...

Putin & I discussed forming an impenetrable Cyber Security unit so that election hacking, & many other negative things, will be guarded.

— 9 July 2017

...only to have to backtrack hours later:

The fact that President Putin and I discussed a Cyber Security unit doesn't mean I think it can happen. It can't-but a ceasefire can,& did!

— 10 July 2017

Many of his tweets are written late at night, when he's clearly half asleep. You can just imagine him lying back on his leopard-skin chaise longue in his dressing gown, eye mask at the ready, his hair draped over the radiator so it can dry out overnight. And just before he drops off, he tweets:

Despite the constant negative press covfefe

— 31 May 2017

This has become one of the most famous of his incoherent late-night tweets. One of his fat orange thumbs must've slipped. Or maybe he's so egomaniacal he thinks he can just invent new words like 'covfefe' and the whole world has to go along with it. After all, Shakespeare invented some terms that are now in common use. And clearly, Trump is a mighty wordsmith on a par with the great bard.

I do understand that people tweet accidently sometimes. Ed Balls knows all about that.[10] But what was great about the 'covfefe' incident was the next day when his then press secretary Sean Spicer was wheeled out to try to convince the press corps that it was an intentional tweet and that the president and a small group of people knew exactly what 'covfefe' meant. Fuck off!

To say that Trump has trouble with spelling and grammar is an immense understatement. To say that his level of literacy is of a kind you'd expect in a community of baboons is closer to the mark. You might say I'm being pedantic or a snob, but these things matter. The man holding the highest office in the Western world *should* care about how he's perceived. He *should* care about high standards of communication and diplomacy. Whenever someone emails me and they can't be bothered to spell my name correctly, it lets me know that they don't really give a shit. A basic spellcheck isn't much of an effort.

This is why every time Trump tweets, he's expressing his contempt for the electorate. He's saying to you, 'I don't need to spell anything correctly. I don't need to consider

---

[10] Former shadow Chancellor Ed Balls got the piss ripped out of him for simply accidentally tweeting his own name and nothing else. He has since spent most of his career trying to top that embarrassing error by losing his seat at the 2015 election and then doing *Strictly Come Dancing*. It didn't work. Ed Balls Day is still celebrated every year on Twitter on 28 April, the anniversary of the tweet. I'm not kidding.

what I'm saying, or how my words might be received. Because your opinion doesn't matter. Nobody's opinion matters but mine.'

Here are some more examples:

Looks to me like the Bernie people will fight. If not, there blood, sweat and tears was a waist of time. Kaine stands for opposite!

– 24 July 2016

How low has President Obama gone to tapp my phones during the very sacred election process. This is Nixon/Watergate. Bad (or sick) guy!

– 4 March 2017

China steals United States Navy research drone in international waters - rips it out of water and takes it to China in unpresidented act

– 17 December 2016

The fact that Twitter is all about brevity can't excuse just how ham-fisted these sentences are. The Gettysburg Address is one of the most profound and memorable speeches in the history of American politics, and Abraham Lincoln managed to convey all that needed to be said in 272 words. I'm not suggesting that Trump could realistically aim to reach Lincoln's standards, but being able to spell 'their', 'waste', 'tap' and 'unprecedented' and knowing when to use a question mark (*hint*: it's after you've asked a question) would be a start.

That's all very well, you might say, but the president's life is a busy one, and he hasn't got time to meticulously check over every single statement he issues. To which I say 'bollocks'. Like every other president, Trump has an army of speechwriters and advisors to help him on these matters. It's just that he chooses not to consult them. He is so arrogant, so entitled, that he believes that he can run the country all by himself and that he can do no wrong,

You'd have thought his tweets would be more articulate given the amount of time it takes him to write them. Have a look at the following two tweets, sent on 5 January 2017:

> *The dishonest media likes saying that I am in Agreement with Julian Assange – wrong. I simply state what he states, it is for the people....*

> *to make up their own minds as to the truth. The media lies to make it look like I am against 'Intelligence' when in fact I am a big fan!*

The first tweet was posted at 5:25am, the second at 5:45am. So even though it's the same sentence, it took him twenty minutes to write the second part. It took him twenty minutes to write thirty words. That's forty seconds a word. And one of those words is 'intelligence'. And some of those words are pretty short. Like 'it' and 'I' and 'the'. It's not like this is sophisticated stuff.

Not that I would dare question the man's intellectual capacity. To those who do, Trump has the following to say:

> *Sorry losers and haters, but my I.Q. is one of the highest -and you all know it! Please don't feel so stupid or insecure,it's not your fault*
>
> *– 8 May 2013*

Trump's lack of self-awareness on Twitter knows no bounds. For example:

> *Truly weird Senator Rand Paul of Kentucky reminds me of a spoiled brat without a properly functioning brain. He was terrible at DEBATE!*
>
> *– 10 August 2015*

Because, of course, when it comes to reasoned debate, this tweet represents the very height of Socratic excellence. Not that he feels the need to debate anyway, since he simply cannot bring himself to even consider that his critics might have a point.

> *Any negative polls are fake news, just like the CNN, ABC, NBC polls in the election. Sorry, people want border security and extreme vetting.*
>
> *– 6 February 2017*

Sensitive souls take note. If your critics upset you, just dismiss them all as liars. It won't make the problem go away, but it'll definitely make you feel better about yourself.

Needless to say, if I were to quote every stupid or ridiculous tweet that Donald Trump has ever issued, this book would end up longer than the Chilcot Report. Just follow him on Twitter. Trust me, it's entertaining and gruesome in equal measure. A bit like *The Walking Dead*.

Twitter allows Trump to dominate the news cycle and as such he has become an almost omnipresent figure. Like Big Brother with a fake tan. Usually, even with the shittest democratic government (the Tories) in charge, it is possible to ignore the news and continue your day without once thinking of Theresa May and her band of merry bastards. But Trump is forever there. In your face. Front page! TV! And his use of Twitter bypasses the press and his behaviour towards, and treatment of, the traditional media is more in line with a regime than a democracy.

One feature of every authoritarian regime in history is that there is only one government-sanctioned media outlet. There can't be competing narratives. And for Trump, apart from his Twitter account, that outlet is Fox News. He wants us to believe that there's Fox News, and there's fake news, and there's nothing in between. It's an effective strategy, which means when the so-called 'fake news' start finding more and more shit on Trump, he'll pretend that they're making it all up, no matter how convincing the evidence. And worse still, his supporters are going to believe him. But opinion is not fake news; it's opinion. Bias is not fake news; it's bias. And thinking Trump is a twat isn't fake news; it's self-evidently true.

Journalists should of course be accountable when they fuck up or lie and should certainly be imprisoned when they break the law. But more importantly, so should the people in power – the politicians, the big corporations – and uncovering corruption is what journalism at its best can do. Let's be in no doubt: that is the sort of journalism Trump is trying to shut down.

This makes reporting on him very tough. To report Trump properly you have to follow him on Twitter.[11] But if he's not on Twitter (i.e., he's golfing), you might want to try the White House daily press briefing. This is where all the journalists in the world sit in an old swimming pool and get shouted at by the White House press secretary. Trump's first press guy, Sean Spicer, recently resigned but trust me, he was a delight. A man so ignorant that he once in a briefing thought it appropriate to refer to Nazi death camps as 'holocaust centres'. What the fuck were the gas chambers? Genocide superstores? Spicer even banned the White House press corps from filming his

---

[11] And not work for Fox News.

press conferences. Which in effect makes a mockery of the whole thing. Scary stuff!

So with a press corps in the White House that isn't fit for purpose your only real way to report Trump is to get an interview with POTUS himself. Even then you're unlikely to get any coherent answers, especially on foreign policy. But if you're lucky you might get a recipe for an amazing chocolate cake.[12]

Even if he does say something of note, be careful. The president is, let's just say, promiscuous with his sources. He would rather quote Fox News over his own national security team, or the FBI, or the CIA. To be fair, most of them are too busy investigating him to be of much use. So your best bet might be to grab a word with one of his top advisors, otherwise known as 'his family'.

Trump's son, Donald Junior recently confirmed that he won't be running for office any time soon. But Trump's daughter is front and centre of the administration.[13] Ivanka recently took the president's seat at the G20 table. There is nothing unusual for a high-ranking official to

---

[12] In one interview, when asked about a US bombing raid in Syria, Trump started talking about the fact that he had recently eaten 'the most beautiful piece of chocolate cake you've ever seen'. He then went on to forget which country he had just bombed.

[13] You can imagine the conversation:
'Daddy, can I have an office in the White House?'
'Sure.'
'Daddy, can you bomb Syria?'
'Anything you say, honey. My God, if you weren't my daughter I'd be grabbing your...'

sit in place of a head of state at such a conference. But for someone with her lack of experience to take that role is unprecedented. She is unelected, has no political or diplomatic experience whatsoever and has her own jewellery range. It's utter madness.

The thing is, this madness would all be over if only someone could get Trump to disclose his tax returns in full. That would be that, and then we can all go back to the good old days. When that big TV show across the pond was a bit more fun. Like that episode when Obama roasted Trump at the correspondent's dinner and tore him a new one.[14] Or like in season 42 when POTUS got caught jizzing on the intern's dress. Now that was good TV!

PART FOUR
Liar-in-Chief

All politicians spin and twist statistics and retract statements and, of course, misspeak from time to time. They also deliberately and consciously renege on election promises they never intended to keep, and when pressed on unsuccessful policies they'll say things like: 'well, in real terms, we have delivered...' In real terms! If ever a politician says the phrase 'in real terms', it means that

---

[14] Chilling viewing these days, given what we now know. This was the moment that Trump decided to get his own back by running for president.

whatever follows hasn't 'really' happened. It's like when they say 'let me be clear'. What they are really saying is 'I am about to lie to you'.[15]

Put simply, most politicians are liars. But when it comes to lies, none of them are as barefaced as Trump's.

Trump in effect kick-started his political career with a lie by accusing Obama of being born in Africa and therefore not eligible to be president. Needless to say, this was an accusation based on no evidence whatsoever. Trump has never conceded he was wrong about that. I don't think he's ever conceded he was wrong about anything, ever. And his administration even made lying acceptable by simply calling it something else: 'alternative facts'.

Even Trump's use of punctuation can have alternative meanings depending what day of the week it is. Take, for instance, the following tweet:

> *Terrible! Just found out that Obama had my "wires tapped" in Trump Tower just before the victory. Nothing found. This is McCarthyism!*

When Sean Spicer was questioned about this outrageous accusation, he argued that Trump's use of quotation marks meant that he didn't actually mean what he said. Even though he'd tweeted the same thing on other occasions without the quotation marks.

---

[15] In the same way, in everyday life if ever someone starts a sentence by saying, 'with the greatest respect', what they really mean is 'fuck off you wanker'.

My personal favourite is Trump's phrase 'truthful hyperbole'. It's an open admission that he likes to exaggerate and twist facts to his own ends. For Trump, reality is what he decides it should be, and it changes from day to day.

The reason why Trump is so brilliant at lying is that he is entirely without shame. He has even said explicitly in press conferences that he isn't going to tell the press everything. He boasts about having secrets.

Like many of us, most politicians are terrified of the embarrassment of being caught in a lie. And, if caught, it's usually that embarrassment that will prompt them to simply apologise and resign. Trump is less concerned with such things. When Trump is caught in a lie he lies further and denies having lied in the first place, which is a lie in itself. So brazen is he with his lies that it's oddly harder to catch him out; his web of lies is just too fucking caked in bullshit to even get near to the truth.

CONCLUSION

The likelihood is that you will not have agreed with every opinion that has been offered within these pages. This is fine. You're not supposed to. This is perfectly normal and is part of human nature.

The human race is full of different colours, creeds, sizes, genders, sexualities, talents and intellectual and physical abilities. Diversity is one of our greatest strengths, and that includes diversity of opinion. If someone offers an opinion that you disagree with, don't worry! More importantly, don't be offended just because somebody thinks or votes differently to you.

Don't avoid different opinions; embrace them. If I see a tweet that I disagree with I'm more inclined to press the follow button than the block button. I like to know what other people are thinking. It is a valuable tool when trying to argue an opposing view. You can't hope to persuade anyone of anything until you can understand their perspective.

With regards to those arguments contained in this book with which you disagree, I would suggest one course of action. Go back and read those sections again. Read them again until you can form an argument that articulates sufficiently why you disagree. Once you've done that, please feel free to pop your thoughts and suggestions on a postcard, stick a second-class stamp on it, and then shove it up your arse.

WHAT'S YOUR
POLITICS?

You are RIGHT-WING if:

- You're related to a barrister.
- You refer to Richard Littlejohn as a 'journalist'.
- You are upset about benefit cheats getting an extra ten pounds per week, but are less concerned with corporations evading millions of pounds worth of tax.
- You've ever eaten a quail's egg.
- You think Enoch Powell was misunderstood.
- When you talk, you occasionally use rhyming hyphenated compounds such as 'fuddy-duddy' (a bit square) or 'rumpy-pumpy' (shagging).
- You don't believe that doctors and nurses are best placed to understand how the NHS works.
- You distrust all these scientists banging on about global warming (you'd much rather rely on your own private hunch than years of training, expertise and research).
- You subscribe to *Tatler* and think that's normal.
- You like nothing better than chasing foxes through the countryside and watching them being torn apart by dogs... whilst drinking port... and thrashing the stable boy... and sleeping with your cousin.

You are LEFT-WING if:

- You consider *The Guardian* to be an impartial newspaper.
- You have an Arts degree.
- You believe in freedom of speech, so long as people agree with you.
- Most of your friends are either vegetarians, vegans or lactose intolerant, which means cooking for the fussy bastards is a nightmare.
- You give money to the homeless (if people are watching).
- You've been using the same Bag-for-Life for over a month.
- You think signing online petitions is political activism.
- You enjoy feeling offended on behalf of minority groups to which you don't actually belong.
- You believe that eating sushi is a cultural appropriation and an insensitive microaggression.
- You're reluctant to debate with anyone who might be more intelligent than you.
- You pretend to like foreign language films.

GLOSSARY

ad hominem

Discrediting someone's argument by making rude or personal comments. For instance, rather than criticising David Cameron for any of his disastrous policy decisions, one might instead simply refer to him as a smug, moon-faced, clammy, gelatinous pigfucker. It might not be very mature, but it is fun.

alt-right

A new right-wing movement in America. It started out as a bunch of bored teenagers trying to piss people off by Internet trolling. Then it attracted fringe groups of white nationalists, who eventually took over. For a while, no one really knew what it meant. But however you define it, you're dealing with dickheads in one form or another.

autocracy

A society in which one individual has all the power. Like North Korea. Or my house during the last six months of my marriage.

backbencher

A member of parliament who sits on the back bench. Not a Cabinet or shadow Cabinet member, who sits on the front bench. You seriously couldn't work that out for yourself?

bigot

A person incapable of accepting that other people have different views than their own. Oddly, the word tends to be used most by those to whom it most applies. So, when a person says that everyone who voted Leave in the EU referendum is a bigot, they are, in fact, being a bigot.

bird-dogging

A hostile media tactic where a reporter will deliberately follow a politician in order to ask them compromising questions. Not to be confused with dogging, which is where lots of sweaty middle-aged men wank over a Honda Civic whilst a couple has sex on the back seats.

Blairite

One who believes fervently in the values of Tony Blair. The clue is in the name, really.

bourgeois

The technical term for the upper middle classes. Or a posh person's way of referring to posh people.

Brexit

Short for 'British exit' in relation to the European Union. When you squash two words together like this it's called a portmanteau. They're normally shit. Like 'Brangelina' or 'Travelodge'. 'Brexit' is made worse by the fact it sounds like a medicine for constipated dogs.

Cabinet

These are the senior ministers who are in charge of the government. The Cabinet comprises the prime minister and (at time of writing) twenty-two other ministers. Some of the roles are highly prestigious, like chancellor of the exchequer, or secretary of state. Others are less so, like secretary of state for transport. Which is a bit like putting one of the slower kids at school in charge of crayons.

Camp David

The US president's official retreat. Also my mate's nickname because he likes Cher.

capitalism

An economic system that prioritises the free market, meaning that trade is a matter for private companies rather than being wholly controlled by the state. In a capitalism system, your worth is judged by how rich you are. Otherwise known as 'the system that fucked our world and turned us all into self-serving pricks'.

centrism

A centrist is one who is neither on the right or left of the political spectrum. Parties often move to the centre in an attempt to appeal to as many people as possible, but all that happens is they end up diluting everything that makes them distinctive. New Labour is a good example of this. See chapter on Tony Blair.

Chequers

The big posh house in Buckinghamshire where the prime minister gets to chill and entertain. And yes, your tax for it.

Chilcot Report

An official report into the Iraq war that confirmed that Tony Blair is a warmongering sociopath incapable of compassion or remorse. Blair rejected the report's findings, which is unsurprising given that he is a warmongering sociopath incapable of compassion or remorse.

Conservatives

The word 'conservative' technically means one who doesn't like things to change. The modern Conservative party was formed in 1834, and it sometimes feels like it's still stuck there. This in itself was a rebrand of the former Tory party, which started in 1678. Most people still refer to them as Tories, because it's quicker and easier to spell. Also, the original meaning of 'Tory' was 'bandit', so that seems quite appropriate given that their *modus operandi* is to steal from the poor to bolster the rich. Like a sick, inverse parody of Robin Hood.

constitution

A list of rules that underpin the values and laws of a country. In the UK, we have an unwritten constitution, which, as you can imagine, is really helpful when it comes to sorting shit out.

coup d'état

A plot to overthrow a government by force. For some reason, this sounds much more sexy in French.

cultural appropriation

The idea that borrowing elements of another's culture is essentially an offensive act. For instance, the students' union at the University of East Anglia recently went about confiscating sombreros from other students on the grounds that they promoted 'discriminatory or stereotypical imagery'. The hats had been given out at a freshers' fair by a local Mexican restaurant.

Sounds like a joke, right? Unfortunately, this kind of thing is now becoming increasingly common on university campuses. Most students are sensible enough to recognise all this stuff as total bullshit, but the vocal and self-righteous minority are the only ones who can be arsed to run for office in the NUS (National Union of Students), so they get to make the rules. These are the killjoys of the future.

So if a British friend puts on a Bob Marley CD, or tries to use chopsticks, or takes up the didgeridoo, make sure you rebuke them in no uncertain terms for their disgusting acts of cultural appropriation. Not that you should be friends with anyone who plays the didgeridoo anyway. Circular breathing does not make you a talented musician.

demagogue

Technically, the word 'demagogue' means 'leader of the people'. But its meaning has changed over the years, and it's now currently used to describe a political figure who avoids rational debate in favour of emotional rhetoric, and likes to appeal to the prejudices of his or her potential voters. People who shout a lot, basically.

democracy

This word comes from the Greek for 'people' (*demos*) and 'rule' (*kratia*). As in, rule of the people. In the UK we have what is called 'parliamentary democracy', through which the people vote and their representatives serve their wishes. This system depends, of course, on politicians living up to the promises made in their manifestos, which doesn't generally happen.

dog whistle

This is a term that's often misused. It refers to coded language used by a politician that is designed to appeal to the few who will understand it. Hence dog whistle, because only dogs can hear it. For instance, when Boris Johnson mentioned Barack Obama's Kenyan heritage, some critics took this as a dog whistle attempt to appeal to racists. I'm saying nothing, because I've got a mortgage to pay and I don't want to be sued.

direct democracy

When the government appeals to the people to make certain decisions. Usually this takes the form of a referendum, sometimes called a plebiscite (literally asking the plebs). A good example of direct democracy in action would be when the Greek government called a referendum to see whether or not its citizens wanted to accept the conditions of austerity imposed by the EU. The people said no. The Greek government and the EU ignored them and went ahead anyway. The Greeks may have invented democracy but they appear to have forgotten what it means.

environmentalism

An important political movement that seeks to protect the planet and its ecosystems for the benefit of future generations. It's often maligned by right-wing politicians who think we should be spending our money on more current concerns. The thing is, the Earth is where we live. It's our home. This is all we've got. We can't just keep trashing the planet in the hope that one day we'll colonise Mars.

Tory governments have repeatedly prioritised short-term economic benefits over the survival of the human race. It doesn't make any fucking sense. How are we going to spend the money if there's nothing left to spend it on? But it's very difficult to get people interested in this stuff because the environment is perceived as being a boring topic. How can we be *bored* of this? We're talking about the destruction of our planet. That's the *opposite* of boring, surely. They make Hollywood films about this kind of shit.

fascism

An ideology that advocates the dictatorial control of the population and economy and the violent suppression of political opposition. The word, however, is commonly misused these days (see chapter on Adolf Hitler). Students at the City University of London, for instance, proposed an 'opposing facism' (*sic*) policy, which led to the ban of certain tabloid newspapers on campus. As you can see, they misspelt the word 'fascism' in their proposal, which explains why the students had been unable to look up its actual definition.

felching

Not a political term at all, but Camp David dared me to put it in the glossary.

filibuster

A tactic whereby a politician talks endlessly in order to delay proceedings in parliament. Often long-winded and deliberately tedious, these speeches are difficult to distinguish from what goes on in parliament on a day-to-day basis.

Filibusters are a mainstay of US politics and are one of the main reasons that nothing ever gets done in Washington.

first-past-the-post

A system of voting in which a majority is not necessarily required. In our parliamentary democracy this means that in a general election, the runner-up can receive many more thousands of votes than the winner.

The same is true in the US, where Hillary Clinton won the popular vote in 2016 by more the 2,500,000 votes. Although that depends on who you ask. Donald Trump vehemently denies this, but that's because he doesn't think facts count for anything.

The first-past-the-post system explains the more curious outcomes of the 2017 general election. The SNP won fifty-six seats from just 4.6 per cent of the vote, as compared to UKIP who had 13 per cent but only emerged with one seat. All of which made us all reflect on the fact that although proportional representation is obviously morally right, there are some plus sides to not living in a true democracy.

gerrymandering

Changing constituencies' boundaries in such a way as to ensure a more favourable outcome. Otherwise known as 'cheating'.

groupthink

A form of herd mentality, where people merely go along with the prevailing norms or trendy opinions without bothering to think for themselves. Otherwise know as 'the human population'.

hack

A word used to describe a shit, derivative journalist. Also the noise my throat makes the morning after a night on the piss.

hate speech

A relatively recent development in UK law that sees people criminalised for saying unpleasant and ignorant things. The problem is that this isn't going to solve anything.

Idiots say idiotic things. That's why we call them idiots. We can't criminalise stupidity. If we did that we'd have to hold a national IQ test and incarcerate the bottom per cent. It's a fucking great idea, but at best is morally dubious.

House of Commons

The first chamber of the UK parliament. It's the important one because the members are actually elected, so we can kick them out if they fuck up. The house is notable for its lack of etiquette.

In debates, the members are encouraged to shout and jeer and generally behave like children. Jeremy Corbyn tried to change all that when he was elected as leader of the Labour Party, but soon backed down when he realised how much fun it was.

House of Lords

The second chamber of the UK parliament. The difference being that these members are not elected. They are usually appointed by a sitting government, so it's often seen as a kind of reward. Not a bad one, either, when you get paid £300 a day just for showing up. Tory peer Baroness Wilcox received more than seventy grand over two years this way, even though she only lives down the road in a house worth four and a half million pounds. It must be very tough for her, all this unrelenting public service.

identity politics

A political movement that sees existence through the prism of groups in society, most typically related to race, nationality, gender and sexuality. All extremely important issues, of course, with the outcome that society has become immeasurably more inclusive.

The problem is that many on the Liberal-Left have focused on identity politics at the expense of the class struggle. The reality is that *money* is all that matters when it comes to inclusivity, social mobility and having the same chances as everyone else. If you're working sixty hours a week on a zero-hour contract and you still can't afford to pay your rent or feed your children, I guarantee your main priority isn't the issues of a sub-Saharan transgender lesbian paraplegic with an eating disorder. You just want to know why you're piss-fuck poor while the rich continue to get richer. You want answers. And no one's giving you those answers, especially the left. So you just get this void where those answers should be, and that vacuum is being filled with right-wing, UKIP-style, 'take back control' rhetoric. And, rightly or wrongly, that is why the left continue to lose.

impeachment

A process that Donald Trump has, at time of writing, somehow bizarrely managed to avoid. Only two presidents have been impeached to date (Nixon doesn't count because he wriggled out of it by resigning before the impeachment process could begin). The first was Andrew Johnson (not to be confused with Lyndon Johnson) in 1868. To be fair to him it was a technicality to do with him breaking a law that was later found to be unconstitutional in and of itself. He was acquitted by the senate. Bill Clinton was impeached, not for getting a blowie in the Oval Office, but for lying about it to a grand jury which, of course, is perjury. He was lucky to get out of that with his presidency intact.

Jeremy Hunt

Rhyming slang for a certain anatomical derogatory term. The real Jeremy Hunt has been secretary of state for health since 2012, and since then has managed to undermine public confidence in the NHS, piss off every junior doctor in the country, and make inroads into the privatisation of the health service by stealth. In short, this is a man who thinks that just because he was born in a hospital means he understands how it works.

Jeremy Hunt is just the latest in a long line of ministers who have attempted to dismantle the NHS and nudge it towards privatisation. It's no good just replacing Hunt, because the problem will just come back again. It's like herpes.

The problem for the Tories is that they can't be seen admitting that they want the NHS to be privatised. They know that it wouldn't go down well with the electorate. So they run it down, make sure it's unmanageable, until privatisation seems like the only option.

What's happened to the NHS under the Tories tells you everything you need to know about the true meaning of austerity. Cut after cut after cut: pile pressure on our public services until those services can only survive in private hands. This is what austerity is. And just because they've stopped using the word doesn't mean it's not austerity. It's not just a word; it's an ideology. And with one hundred and fifty avoidable deaths a week in our hospitals it's an ideology that kills people. Theresa May recently rebranded austerity as 'living within our means', but what's the point of living within your means if you're dead?

Let's face it, entrusting the Tories with our NHS is about as sensible as cleaning your dog's teeth with your bellend.

jingoism

A fancy word for patriotism. Don't use it. You'll sound like a twat.

kleptocracy

This word literally means 'rule by thieves'. It applies to any society that is run by corrupt, self-interested bureaucrats. Most of them, then.

Labour

For centuries there had been no party in parliament willing to look out for the needs of the working class. Then in 1900 along came Labour, a new party that brought together trade unions and workers who would provide a voice for the downtrodden in parliament. The socialist experiment worked to an extent, as it is Labour governments that have been responsible for the welfare state, equal opportunities and the NHS. Not bad going.

For a while there, Labour went rogue under Tony Blair, abandoned socialism, and become 'New Labour' (see chapter on Tony Blair). The 2017 Labour manifesto changed all that, and with Jeremy Corbyn at the helm we have a socialist back in charge. Given that Labour is meant to be a socialist party, you'd think more people would be happy about it.

laissez-faire economics

An economic system that allows private businesses to trade without intervention from the government. It also means a relaxed and chilled view towards certain things. Unfortunately, it is usually used when talking about things like trade regulations, workers' rights and social care.

Liberal Democrats

In 1988 the Liberal Party and the Social Democratic Party merged to form the Liberal Democrats. A bit like when McFly and Busted merged to form McBusted.

liberalism

A philosophy rooted in the concept of human equality. As such, secularism (separation of church and state), freedom of speech, press freedom and civil rights are fundamental values. In 'classic liberalism' this becomes entwined with market freedom and laissez-faire economics. Liberals hate the wrong sort of liberal. In fact, at present there are probably more illiberal liberals than liberal liberals.

Liberal-Left

A sort of ugly crossover between the left and liberalism, invariably focusing on issues of race, gender and sexuality rather than issues of class. So, if you're a straight white male you are considered the most privileged person on the planet, even if you're on unemployment benefit and can't afford to wash. The 'Liberal-Left' are also terrified of people disagreeing with them, so have a tendency to oppose freedom of speech in the name of promoting equality. Another word for this is 'hypocrisy'.

libertarian

One who believes that the state should have as little involvement as possible in the affairs of the individual citizen. This gets quite complicated because there are *economic libertarians*, who don't much like taxation or the state intervening when they are making obscene amounts of money. Then there are *cultural libertarians* who don't think it's the state's job to police people's private lives, thoughts, speech, or anything else they happen to enjoy which doesn't infringe on the rights of others. Cultural libertarians have a good point. Economic libertarians, by contrast, are generally scum.

Magna Carta

This means 'great charter' in Latin and was a binding agreement that King John was forced to sign in 1215, effectively restricting the powers of the monarch. It's a founding document of Western democracy, insofar as it ensures that even leaders are not above the law. It also enshrined the principle of a fair trial for all citizens, which is why we all hold so dear the idea of 'innocent until proven guilty'. Except when it comes to *The Sun* newspaper, who prefer the creed of 'guilty if they look a bit dodgy, until we have to retract it in small print after the case is dropped'.

mansplaining

A rude and patronising term to help explain the phenomenon of a man interrupting a woman and explaining things to her in a rude and patronising manner. It's another example of regressive left-wing bullshit that does nothing to help the feminist cause and everything to further the narrative that women are weak and need protection from the real world.

Yes, some men are sexist and misogynistic. I am not.

If I am explaining something to you in a rude and patronising manner, it will not be because you are a woman. It will be because you're a fucking cretin. Your gender will have nothing to do with it. I am rude and patronising to everyone. I'm a big believer in equal rights. If you require special treatment because you are a woman then fuck off back to the 1940s.

Mike Pence

The US's most likely next president. Satan in human form.

monarchy

An archaic system in which one family are afforded incredible prestige, power and wealth on the basis of an accident of birth. And even though the current queen has no real say when it comes to running the country, there's something ever so slightly perverse about the idea of paying millions of pounds of taxpayers' money annually to a woman who is already worth £277 million. The typical monarchist argument goes along the lines of 'Yes, but the royal family are good for tourism'. Well, so is Chester Zoo, but we don't buy private jets for the gibbons.

neoliberalism

It sounds good doesn't it? New Liberalism! Do not be deceived. 'Neoliberalism' is one of those catch-all phrases that is often misused. It's liberalism when applied to economics. It's that laissez-faire thing again that prioritises the free market, shifting control from the public sector to the private sector. When most people say 'neoliberalism' they basically mean 'capitalism' but want to sound more sophisticated.

New Labour

Centre-right politicians pretending to be socialists. See chapter on Tony Blair.

partisan

Aligned very strongly to a particular political ideology. Like every single fucking newspaper ever.

political correctness

Otherwise known as 'PC'. This started out as a good idea, encouraging people to be polite to each other, e.g., not referring to gay people as 'faggots'. The culture of offence that has since developed is not quite the same thing as political correctness, it's a weird perversion of it which is used to find offence where there is none, to shut down arguments based upon a person's perceived privilege, to justify censorship and to crack down on freedom of speech.

proportional representation

A system by which everyone's vote actually counts. You know, otherwise known as 'democracy'. We haven't quite reached that point yet.

queer

A term relating to sexual politics. Those who identify as 'queer' do so because they want an ambiguous label that indicates their sexual non-conformity (which is odd, because there are so many of them).

'Queer' is a good example of how words change their meanings over time. It used to be a word to describe anything remotely odd. So, if a man were to say, 'Goodness me, Horace, your dog is a little queer', this would not in any way imply that Horace's dog had homosexual inclinations, but merely that the dog was odd in some way.

Later, 'queer' became a derogatory term for gay people. 'Queer-bashing' became a pastime for thugs, especially in the years that followed the decriminalisation of homosexuality in 1967. In order to diffuse the power of those who sought to denigrate them, gay people reclaimed the term for themselves.

So the word has shifted from being an innocuous adjective, to a pejorative term of abuse, to a positive form of self-identification. All in the space of two generations. This is why older people struggle to keep up. When your nan refers to people of colour as 'coloureds', it might be worth considering whether she is using the phrase because she is unaware in shifts in acceptable language, rather than because she is an out-and-out racist.

'Queer', then, has now become pretty mainstream. It's the 'Q' in the phrase 'LGBTQIA+'. And if that phrase gets any longer I swear we're going to have to extend the alphabet in order to cope.

racial profiling

Technically illegal, this is a process whereby people are more likely to be investigated on the basis of their race. Like when airport security stop and search someone who looks suspiciously brown.

realpolitik

A German word that means 'realistic politics'. It's when morality is ditched in favour of practical concerns, a political approach where the head rules over the heart.

Truman's decision to drop the atomic bomb is a fine example of *realpolitik* in action.

safe space

Not a literal space as such, but rules that are applied to ensure that people won't have to encounter any views or ideas that make them uncomfortable. Safe Spaces are common on university campuses, but less so in the real world.

Trotskyite

An offensive term for a Trotskyist.

Trotskyist

A nicer term for a Trotskyite.

utilitarianism

The idea that decisions should be made on the basis of whether or not the outcome produces the greatest good for the greatest number. Probably best defined by Spock in *Star Trek II: The Wrath of Khan*: 'Logic clearly dictates that the needs of the many outweigh the needs of the few'.

vox *populi*

A fancy Latin term for 'voice of the people', which is used when needing to express what the common folk believe. In my job, this term is often shortened to 'vox pop', and means an interview with a member of the general public. I try to avoid them, because they always come out with utter shit.

whip

The disciplinarian in any given political party. This is the person who threatens MPs to vote the 'right' way. I've always felt this would be much more effective if he or she could be armed with an actual whip.

Xanthippe

The name of Socrates' wife. Socrates was one of the key founders of Western philosophy, and his theories underpin the modern method of political debate.

This entry is properly tenuous, I know. But I've got OCD and I had to include at least one word for every letter of the alphabet in this glossary. If I didn't, the world might explode or something.

yield gap

In economics, a method of comparing bonds and shares. Boring, I know, but what the fuck else begins with Y?

zip wire

That thing Boris got stuck on. Twat!

Soul *Retreats*™

_____

Presented To

_____

Presented By

_____

Date

Soul Retreats™ for Leaders
ISBN 0-310-80185-0

Copyright 2005 by GRQ Ink, Inc.
Franklin, Tennessee 37067
"Soul Retreats" is a trademark owned by GRQ, Inc.

Published by Inspirio™, The gift group of Zondervan
5300 Patterson Avenue, SE
Grand Rapids, Michigan 49530

Requests for information should be addressed to:
Inspirio™, The gift group of Zondervan
Grand Rapids, Michigan 49530

http://www.inspiriogifts.com

Editor and Compiler: Lila Empson
Associate Editor: Janice Jacobson
Project Manager: Tom Dean
Manuscript written by Melinda Mahand
    Whisner Design Group

Soul Retreats™
for Leaders

Contents

1. A Purposeful Calling (Destiny)....................8

2. Vision Restored (Focus) 12

3. Taking the Next Step (Perseverance) 16

4. What Do You Think? (Mind Renewal) 20

5. A Clear Objective (Purpose)........................24

6. The Place to Begin (Prayer)........................28

7. He's Got You Covered (Security)..................32

8. All in the Attitude (Joy) 36

9. Constant and True (Confidence) 40

10. Wonderful Counselor (God's Word) 44

11. Light in the Darkness (Challenging Times) 48

12. Good Intentions (Grace) 52

13. An Arm of Strength (Power)........................56

14. Picking Up the Pieces (Prayer) 60

15. When the Going Gets Tough (Determination)........64

16. When God Chooses (Humility) 68

17. True Leadership (Mentoring) 72

18. Access Offered (Wisdom) 76

19. An Unexpected Power (Gentleness) 80

20. The Door to Success (Hard Work) 84

21. Training for the Task (Discipline) 88

22. Look to the Outcome (Adversity) 92

23. What Do You Know? (Knowing God) 96

24. Never Alone (God's Presence) 100

25. The Hard Choice (Courage) 104

26. Desire Fulfilled (Satisfaction) 108

27. Weightlifters (Kindness) 112

28. Made of Bedrock (Integrity) 116

29. Finding a Fresh Start (Forgiveness) 120

30. Multiplied Blessing (Giving) 124

Introduction

Your leadership role requires a
demanding combination of managerial,
supervisory, and leadership skills that
sometimes invigorate and sometimes challenge you physically,
mentally, and spiritually. *Soul Retreats™ for Leaders* is a tool to
renew your energy and restore your soul.

Each selection encourages you to suspend the demands on
your time and energy for a few minutes of the day. Each leads you
to use this time to communicate with God and to focus on effective
skills and techniques for fulfilling your leadership responsibilities.
In addition, each directs you to receive renewed vision, purpose,
and motivation from the Lord.

Browse through the retreat titles and choose each day the
selection that interests you, or simply read the retreats in the order
they appear. Either way, you will discover encouragement,
strength, and insight directed specifically to you as a leader.

Every Soul Has a Purpose

Everyone who breathes has a mission, has a work.
We are not sent into this world for nothing;
we are not here, that we may go to bed at night,
and get up in the morning, toil for our bread, rear a family and die.
God sees every one of us;
He creates every soul for a purpose.

John Henry Newman

A Purposeful Calling

Step away from the people and tasks vying for your attention. Let go of concerns about appointments on your calendar or messages in your voice mail. Take the time now to quiet inner demands and allow yourself a few minutes to consider an important topic—your destiny, what is to happen to fulfill your life's purpose.

The constant press of time often can obscure the question of your destiny. As a leader, you are consumed with intricately planning the moments and mandates of your days, and you may easily find yourself caught up in whirlwinds of activity that kick up a stir but head nowhere. You may have little time to consider whether your pursuits are on a parallel path with your calling.

In this fast-paced culture, the people who have the farthest reaching influence, who make the longest lasting impact, are those who are intimately aware of their personal calling. These leaders recognize they are to spend their lives in pursuits that make eternal investments.

Use this time to consider your personal calling, to consider scheduling your activities by chosen priorities rather than by insistent demands, and to consider where you can find meaning and purpose for your endeavors.

Leaders possess a sense of destiny—a personal belief that they are meant for something special, perhaps even greatness.
—Donald T. Phillips

A Moment to Reflect

God created your days and has a plan for your use of them. He cares about the pressures and stresses you face, and he also sees beyond this moment. He knows where you are and where you are going, and his calling provides meaning for them both.

Ask God to show you the things he has called you to do. Ask him for direction to recognize which tasks to accept and which ones to lay aside without regret or guilt. Thank him for bringing you this far and for continuing to be your guide. Thank God for designing your destiny and for setting before you the tasks that lie ahead of you.

Be inspired with the belief that life is a great and noble calling; not a mean and groveling thing that we are to shuffle through as we can, but an elevated and lofty destiny.

—WILLIAM E. GLADSTONE

9

*The one who calls you is faithful
and he will do it.*

1 Thessalonians 5:24 NIV

A Moment to Refresh

*All things are done according to God's plan
and decision; and God chose us to be his own
people in union with Christ because of his own
purpose, based on what he had decided from the
very beginning.*

Ephesians 1:11 GNT

*O LORD, you are my God; I will exalt you,
I will praise your name; for you have done
wonderful things, plans formed of old,
faithful and sure.*

Isaiah 25:1 NRSV

*I pray also that the eyes of your heart may be
enlightened in order that you may know the
hope to which he has called you, the riches of
his glorious inheritance in the saints, and his
incomparably great power for us who believe.
That power is like the working of his mighty
strength.*

Ephesians 1:18–19 NIV

In our calling, we have to choose; we must make our fortune either in this world or in the next, there is no middle way.

—MARIE HENRI BEYLE

"I know the plans I have for you," declares the LORD, "plans to prosper you and not to harm you, plans to give you hope and a future."

Jeremiah 29:11 NIV

He who began a good work in you will carry it on to completion until the day of Christ Jesus.

Philippians 1:6 NIV

It is God himself who makes us, together with you, sure of our life in union with Christ; it is God himself who has set us apart, who has placed his mark of ownership upon us, and who has given us the Holy Spirit in our hearts as the guarantee of all that he has in store for us.

2 Corinthians 1:21–22 GNT

Life is a privilege, a responsibility, a stewardship to be lived according to a much higher calling, God's calling. This alone gives true meaning to life.

—ELIZABETH DOLE

Vision Restored

A Moment to Pause

How many ways have your eyes been useful today? Perhaps they helped you maneuver through rush–hour traffic, analyze information on a computer screen, or interpret the body language of another person. In each of these instances, blurry vision could easily have caused difficulty and possibly even led to critical error. Such improper focus would have prompted you to seek medical help or corrective lenses to restore your vision.

In addition to physical eyesight, you have another type of vision as well, the vision called faith, which enables you to view life through spiritual eyes. The difference from physical is that spiritual vision comprehends things not seen.

Just as physical eyes sometimes lose their focus, spiritual eyes can do so as well. When you look only on the circumstances of the moment instead of viewing events from an eternal perspective, God's ultimate purposes can become blurry and discouragement can ensue. Likewise, when you concentrate only on the long–range desired outcome of your endeavors, the importance of maintaining integrity each step of the way may become blurred, and you could discourage those who follow you.

Fortunately, God can renew both your faith and your focus when you turn to him for restoration.

*God has made for us two kinds of eyes: those of
flesh and those of faith.*

—SAINT JOHN CHRYSOSTOM

A Moment to Reflect

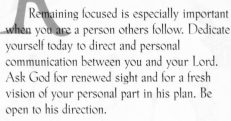

Remaining focused is especially important when you are a person others follow. Dedicate yourself today to direct and personal communication between you and your Lord. Ask God for renewed sight and for a fresh vision of your personal part in his plan. Be open to his direction.

When God begins to restore your sight, recognize that this vision is a precursor of your duty. Few are called to contemplation and reflection only. God provides vision to strengthen and prepare his leaders for action. Those who have by faith seen and believed the most will by faith do the most.

Blind trust in God promises
a focus sharper than circumstance,
an image clearer than emotion,
an insight purer than advice.
The Bible calls it faith, for it is confidence;
the Bible calls it hope, for it is the expectation;
we did not see, and yet believed.

✌

—MELINDA MAHAND

13

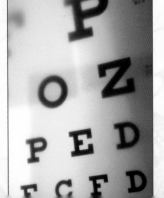

We fix our eyes not on what is seen, but on what is unseen. For what is seen is temporary, but what is unseen is eternal.

2 Corinthians 4:18 NIV

A Moment to Refresh

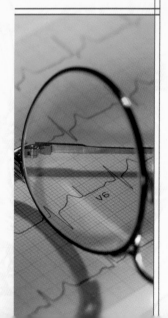

We walk by faith, not by sight.

2 Corinthians 5:7 KJV

Let us fix our eyes on Jesus, the author and perfecter of our faith, who for the joy set before him endured the cross, scorning its shame, and sat down at the right hand of the throne of God. Consider him who endured such opposition from sinful men, so that you will not grow weary and lose heart

Hebrews 12:2–3 NIV

Faith is being sure of what we hope for and certain of what we do not see.

Hebrews 11:1 NIV

I lift up my eye to the hills—where does my help come from? My help comes from the LORD, the Maker of heaven and earth.

Psalm 121:1–2 NIV

A vision without a task is a dream; a task without a vision is drudgery; a vision and a task is the hope of the world.

—AUTHOR UNKNOWN

The precepts of the LORD are right, giving joy to the heart. The commands of the LORD are radiant, giving light to the eyes.

Psalm 19:8 NIV

The eye is the lamp of the body. If your eyes are good, your whole body will be full of light.

Matthew 6:22 NIV

Jesus said, "Everything is possible for the person who has faith."

Mark 9:23 GNT

Be on your guard; stand firm in the faith; be men of courage; be strong. Do everything in love.

1 Corinthians 16:13–14 NIV

It is the peculiar business of faith's eye to see in the dark.

—AUGUSTUS M. TOPLADY

Taking the Next Step

A Moment to Pause

Retreat today to a place of quietness where you can stop to refresh your soul. Take a moment to look around the room for symbols of the success stories in your life. Perhaps your eye will pause on a photo of your family, a plaque of commendation, or some other memento of your commitment toward a goal. Were any of these successes achieved easily? They most likely were not, for great success usually comes only at the expense of unflinching perseverance.

Nature consistently teaches the rewards of perseverance. Consider, for instance, the example of the caterpillar and the grasshopper. The caterpillar is not discouraged by its slow pace when the grasshopper covers a comparatively great distance in a single leap. The caterpillar does not give up because its legs are not as muscular and its movements seemingly less successful. Instead the caterpillar walks faithfully on, step after step after step after step. And one day that tiny insect will receive a reward for its perseverance.

As a transformed creature it will emerge from its chrysalis, discover delicate new wings, and loft gracefully into the sky—leaving the grasshopper still jumping up and down. Unflinching perseverance has its rewards.

The vision must be followed by the venture. It is not enough to stare up the steps—we must step up the stairs.

—VANCE HAVNER

A Moment to Reflect

What keeps a person persistently moving toward his goal, even when the pathway becomes toilsome and each step becomes a challenge? Unwavering hope, an inner reservoir of strength, the promise of ultimate reward—these are the pillars of perseverance, and they infuse the person who encounters difficulties and yet moves on.

You can renew the pillars of hope, strength, and reward in your life by turning to the encouragement of God's Word. The Scripture passages on the following pages offer a good place to begin. Each verse will offer you a reason to hope, a restoration of strength, and a promise of reward. Claim them in your life today—and then take your next step.

There are but two roads that lead to an important goal and to the doing of great things: strength and perseverance. Strength is the lot of but a few privileged men; but austere perseverance, harsh and continuous, may be employed by the smallest of us and rarely fails of its purpose, for its silent power grows irresistibly greater with time.

—JOHANN WOLFGANG VON GOETHE

Those who hope in the LORD will renew their strength. They will soar on wings like eagles; they will run and not grow weary, they will walk and not be faint.

Isaiah 40:31 NIV

A Moment to Refresh

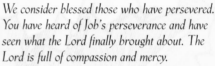

We consider blessed those who have persevered. You have heard of Job's perseverance and have seen what the Lord finally brought about. The Lord is full of compassion and mercy.

James 5:11 NIV

May you be made strong with all the strength which comes from his glorious power, so that you may be able to endure everything with patience.

Colossians 1:11 GNT

We also rejoice in our sufferings, because we know that suffering produces perseverance; perseverance, character; and character, hope.

Romans 5:3–4 NIV

Everything that was written in the past was written to teach us, so that through endurance and the encouragement of the Scriptures we might have hope.

Romans 15:4 NIV

By perseverance the snail reached the ark.

—CHARLES HADDON SPURGEON

Consider it pure joy, my brothers, whenever you face trials of many kinds, because you know that the testing of your faith develops perseverance. Perseverance must finish its work so that you may be mature and complete, not lacking anything.
James 1:2–4 NIV

Love is patient, love is kind. It does not envy, it does not boast, it is not proud. It is not rude, it is not self–seeking, it is not easily angered, it keeps no record of wrongs. Love does not delight in evil but rejoices with the truth. It always protects, always trusts, always hopes, always perseveres. Love never fails.
1 Corinthians 13:4–8 NIV

Blessed is the man who perseveres under trial, because when he has stood the test, he will receive the crown of life that God has promised to those who love him.
James 1:12 NIV

We conquer—not in any brilliant fashion—we conquer by continuing.

—GEORGE MATHESON

What Do You Think?

A Moment to Pause   Step away from the responsibilities and decisions that clamor for your attention. Take a few moments to gather your thoughts and renew your mind. Because you are a person in a position of influence, people try to read your mind each day. They try to uncover your thoughts with such questions as "What do you suggest?" "What's your opinion?" "What would you do?" or "What do you think?"

Your thoughts determine your choices, your actions, and your attitudes. What is more, right thoughts can produce right choices, right actions, and right attitudes. When your heart is right with God through prayer and seeking to do his will, when your thinking is true to biblical principles through the thoughtful study of Scripture, then your conduct is based upon the right standard and is directed to the right end.

Not every thought, of course, is right and true. God invites you to renew your mind with his Word, to put your thoughts into right relation to things infinite and eternal in order to acquire the faculty of accurate discernment and wise judgment. When your mind is renewed, as your spirit has been, your thoughts can become decisive, productive, and inspiring to many.

Power lasts ten years;
influence not more than a hundred.
—KOREAN PROVERB

A Moment to Reflect

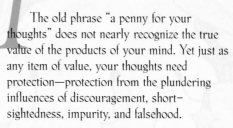

The old phrase "a penny for your thoughts" does not nearly recognize the true value of the products of your mind. Yet just as any item of value, your thoughts need protection—protection from the plundering influences of discouragement, short-sightedness, impurity, and falsehood.

Commit your mind to God today, for he is Lord of all that is good—good ideas, noble impulses, and powerful inspirations. Marauding thoughts may still invade your mind from time to time, but do not be dismayed. You may not be able to choose every thought that enters your mind, but you can choose which ones you invite to move in and maintain residence.

Change my mind, Lord.
When thoughts are pensive, give me peace.
When weary, give me rest.
When fearful, give me strength
and courage for the test.
When my heart is swayed by any thought
that isn't for my best,
change my mind, Lord.

༄

—Melinda Mahand

21

The thoughts of the righteous are right: but the counsels of the wicked are deceit.

Proverbs 12:5 KJV

A Moment to Refresh

Fill your minds with those things that are good and that deserve praise: things that are true, noble, right, pure, lovely, and honorable. Put into practice what you learned and received from me, both from my words and from my actions. And the God who gives us peace will be with you.

Philippians 4:8–9 GNT

Search me, O God, and know my heart; test me and know my anxious thoughts. See if there is any offensive way in me, and lead me in the way everlasting.

Psalm 139:23–24 NIV

Thou wilt keep him in perfect peace, whose mind is stayed on thee: because he trusteth in thee.

Isaiah 26:3 KJV

What we think about when we are free to think about what we will—that is what we are or will soon become.

—A. W. Tozer

Do not conform any longer to the pattern of this world, but be transformed by the renewing of your mind. Then you will be able to test and approve what God's will is—his good, pleasing and perfect will.

Romans 12:2 NIV

We demolish arguments and every pretension that sets itself up against the knowledge of God, and we take captive every thought to make it obedient to Christ.

2 Corinthians 10:5 NIV

Those who live according to the sinful nature have their minds set on what that nature desires; but those who live in accordance with the Spirit have their minds set on what the Spirit desires. The mind of sinful man is death, but the mind controlled by the Spirit is life and peace.

Romans 8:5–6 NIV

At every point right living begins with right thinking.

—Bruce Milne

A Clear Objective

A Moment to Pause

Allow yourself a few moments of quiet solitude today, a time to restore and refocus. Realize that such moments are not a waste of time. Realize that they are an investment that enables you to better use the rest of your day.

Your time is in great demand. A wide variety of tasks request your attention, many more than you could personally attend to. A large part of your success is your learning which tasks to pursue and which ones to decline or delegate.

Understanding God's purposes in your life is the key to making these crucial decisions. Just as each tool on your desktop is designed for a specific task, so you are a tool as well, a tool individually designed by God for his purposes. He created each facet of your being with his end in mind.

Much like the people who work under you who need your leadership and guidance to understand their responsibilities, you, too, need to submit to the One above you. You need direction from God in order to maintain a clear vision of his objectives. God's purposes are higher than man's, and higher purposes require a higher power, a power that God alone can provide.

The two greatest days in a person's life are the
day he was born and the day he finds out
why he was born.

—Author Unknown

A Moment to Reflect

Recognize today that God's divine purpose will not be turned aside by some fault found in an individual character. Noah failed in some instances. So did Abraham and Moses and David. The stories of these individuals are significant, not because they never stumbled, but because God worked through them in spite of their frailties and shortcomings. God's purposes were fulfilled.

You, too, were born for a definite purpose and can live a life of significance. Take your eyes off yourself, and set them on God. Look higher and reach higher, and you will find both your purpose and his power.

The main thing in this world is not being sure what God's will is, but seeking it sincerely, and following what we do understand of it. The only possible answer to the destiny of man is to seek without respite to fulfill God's purpose.

—PAUL TOURNIER

25

*As the heavens are higher than the earth, so
are my ways higher than your ways and my
thoughts than your thoughts.*

Isaiah 55:9 NIV

A Moment to Refresh

*I press on toward the goal to win the prize for
which God has called me heavenward in
Christ Jesus.*

Philippians 3:14 NIV

*In Christ we have also obtained an inheritance,
having been destined according to the purpose of
him who accomplishes all things according to
his counsel and will.*

Ephesians 1:11 NRSV

*The LORD who rules over all has taken an oath.
He has said, "You can be sure that what I have
planned will happen. What I have decided will
take place." . . . The LORD who rules over all
has planned it. Who can stop him? He has
reached out his powerful hand. Who can keep
him from using it?*

Isaiah 14:24, 27 NIRV

The all-important aim in Christian meditation is to allow God's mysterious and silent presence within us to become more and more not only a reality, but ... that reality which gives meaning and shape and purpose to everything we do; to everything we are.

—JOHN MAIN

I cry out to God Most High, to God, who fulfills his purpose for me.

Psalm 57:2 NIV

To everything there is a season, and a time to every purpose under the heaven.

Ecclesiastes 3:1 KJV

We know that in all things God works for the good of those who love him, who have been called according to his purpose.

Romans 8:28 NIV

The LORD *will fulfill his purpose for me; your love, O* LORD, *endures forever—do not abandon the works of your hands.*

Psalm 138:8 NIV

The world stands aside to let anyone pass who knows where he is going.

—AUTHOR UNKNOWN

The Place to Begin

Whether you are preparing to begin your day or finally drawing it to a close, claim a few minutes as your own just now. As you begin to relax, recall a moment in your life when you achieved that coveted title of "winner." Recall the energizing thrill, the surge of satisfaction, the moment of sheer glory. Whether the finish line you crossed was a mark in the sand or a lofty goal on a corporate chart, winning is a great and memorable experience. Yet on a professional course, the finish line is not the only point that needs consideration. Professional competitors know that years of rigorous training precede the beginning of any race. Crossing the finish line is a result of that preparation.

Your professional endeavors are similar. You need to focus steadily on the course that lies before you as well as to have a clear vision of the finish line. But you need more. If you want your leadership to have a dynamic impact, you must begin with prayer.

Prayer helps you put your thoughts into words. It allows you to seek God's guidance and his blessing. Prayer is a significant part of the behind-the-scenes work that goes into making a plan work.

Prayer should be short, without giving God Almighty reasons why he should grant this or that; he knows best what is good for us.
—JOHN SELDEN

28

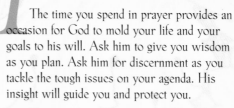

A Moment to Reflect

The time you spend in prayer provides an occasion for God to mold your life and your goals to his will. Ask him to give you wisdom as you plan. Ask him for discernment as you tackle the tough issues on your agenda. His insight will guide you and protect you.

Determine to make prayer the first step in each new endeavor of life. As amazing as it may seem, God promises to listen and, even more amazingly, he promises to answer. Take a few moments to talk to him now. Prayer is always the best place to begin.

The greatest thing anyone can do for God and for man is to pray. You can do more than pray after you have prayed, but you cannot do more than pray until you have prayed.

—S. D. GORDON

I love the LORD, for he heard my voice; he heard my cry for mercy. Because he turned his ear to me, I will call on him as long as I live.

Psalm 116: 1–2 NIV

A Moment to Refresh

You answer us with awesome deeds of righteousness, O God our Savior, the hope of all the ends of the earth and of the farthest seas, who formed the mountains by your power, having armed yourself with strength.

Psalm 65:5–6 NIV

Do not be anxious about anything, but in everything, by prayer and petition, with thanksgiving, present your requests to God. And the peace of God, which transcends all understanding, will guard your hearts and your minds in Christ Jesus.

Philippians 4:6–7 NIV

I call on you, O God, for you will answer me; give ear to me and hear my prayer. Show the wonder of your great love, you who save by your right hand those who take refuge in you from their foes.

Psalm 17:6–7 NIV

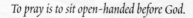

To pray is to sit open-handed before God.

⋟

—Peter G. van Breeman

Jesus said, "Is there anyone among you who, if your child asks for bread, will give a stone? Or if the child asks for a fish, will give a snake? If you then, who are evil, know how to give good gifts to your children, how much more will your Father in heaven give good things to those who ask him!"

Matthew 7:9–11 NRSV

Jesus said, "I tell you the truth, my Father will give you whatever you ask in my name."

John 16:23 NIV

Answer me, O LORD, out of the goodness of your love; in your great mercy turn to me. Do not hide your face from your servant; answer me quickly, for I am in trouble.

Psalm 69:16–17 NIV

Prayer can do anything God can do.

⋟

—E. M. Bounds

He's Got You Covered

A Moment to Pause

As you retreat temporarily from the day's demands, invite your thoughts to dwell on images that give you a sense of protection and security. Chances are good that the images involve some type of physical covering, for a covering by its very function offers protection. Your organization or business, for example, has governing policies that cover various aspects of operation in order to protect the employees as well as the business itself.

When the Bible says that God is a shield, a tower, or shelter, it is addressing your most basic need for safety and protection. The selection of those images of God is meant to assure you that you are defended on every side and that in the shelter of his covering you are completely secure.

People sometimes respond to the conflicts of life by turning elsewhere for defense. They may count on the sufficiency of intellect, the support of friends, the adequacy of personal strength or personal finances, or perhaps merely the power of their own endurance.

Placing your need for security in the hands of anyone or anything other than God, however, soon results in paralyzing feelings of anxiety, weariness, tension, or even outright fear.

Security is not the absence of danger, but the presence of God, no matter what the danger.

—AUTHOR UNKNOWN

A Moment to Reflect The covering that protects you is God's own omnipotence. His protection can provide you with the strength to lead others, the wisdom to sort through difficult decisions, and the peace to lead others with confidence.

As you read the verses on the next few pages, look for words that describe the type of covering or protection that God provides. Spend a few moments meditating on the security each description offers you personally and how that security enables you to lead more effectively. Then thank him and go forward with confidence. As the saying goes, he's got you covered.

Do not look forward to the changes and chances of this life in fear; rather look to them with full hope that, as they arise, God, whose you are, will deliver you out of them. He is your keeper. He has kept you hitherto. Do you but hold fast to his dear hand, and he will lead you safely through all things.

—*Saint Francis de Sales*

Surely, O LORD, you bless the righteous;
you surround them with your favor as
with a shield.

Psalm 5:12 NIV

A Moment to Refresh

The name of the Lord is a strong tower; The
righteous runs into it and is safe.

Proverbs 18:10 NASB

The LORD is my rock, my fortress, and my
deliverer, my God, my rock, in whom I take
refuge, my shield and the horn of my salvation,
my stronghold and my refuge, my savior; you
save me from violence. I call upon the LORD,
who is worthy to be praised, and I am saved
from my enemies.

2 Samuel 22:2–4 NRSV

When I am afraid, I will trust in you. In God,
whose word I praise, in God I trust; I will not
be afraid. What can mortal man do to me?

Psalm 56:3–4 NIV

It is the LORD who goes before you. He will be
with you; he will not fail you or forsake you.
Do not fear or be dismayed.

Deuteronomy 31:8 NRSV

*This is a wise, sane Christian faith: that a man commits himself,
his life, and his hopes to God; that God undertakes the special
protection of that man; that therefore that man ought not to be
afraid of anything.*

—GEORGE MACDONALD

Jesus said, "In the world you have
tribulation, but take courage; I have
overcome the world."

John 16:33 NASB

God will cover you with his wings. Under
the feathers of his wings you will find safety.
He is faithful. He will keep you safe like a
shield or a tower. . . . The LORD is the one
who keeps you safe. So let the Most High
God be like a home to you.

Psalm 91:4, 9 NIRV

*Be still my soul: the
Lord is on thy side.*

—KATHARINA VON
SCHLEGEL

God holds victory in store for the upright,
he is a shield to those whose walk is
blameless, for he guards the course
of the just and protects the way of his
faithful ones.

Proverbs 2:7–8 NIV

All in the Attitude

A Moment to Pause

Put on hold for a few minutes the people and tasks vying for your attention. Focus your thoughts on your attitude toward those people and tasks. Ask yourself whether you are continuing to find joy in your role as a leader. This joyful outlook is an important tool for maintaining your effectiveness. Joy is a powerful force to motivate and strengthen both you and the ones you lead. Joy promotes endurance and increases fulfillment, and it reveals great inner constancy and power. Today you can plug into this power by making the choice to undergo a simple attitude adjustment.

To begin, understand the difference between joy and happiness. Happiness is an emotional response to outward circumstances. Certain occurrences make you feel happy while others do not. Joy is an attitude that results when you make the conscious choice to trust God with the circumstances and occurrences in your life. Happiness is a feeling; joy is a choice.

When you possess a confident awareness that God is working all things together for your good, your attitude incorporates an inner joy, whether your eyes clearly see his plan, whether your mind comprehends his purposes, or whether your feelings match up with his promises.

*Happiness depends on what happens;
joy does not.*
—OSWALD CHAMBERS

A Moment to Reflect

Having an attitude of joy does not mean you will never experience feelings of sadness. But you can be hurt or frustrated with an event in your life and still make the conscious choice to hold on to an inner attitude of joy—not in the circumstance itself, but in the God who works in, through, and even in spite of your circumstance.

Examine your attitude for a moment. Are you choosing to place your trust in God? Are you choosing to believe his promise that he is actively working for your good? Make any necessary attitude adjustments as you read this, and then go forward with joy into the rest of your day.

Happiness is caused by things that happen around me, and circumstances will mar it; but joy flows right on through trouble; joy flows in the night as well as in the day; joy flows through persecution and opposition. It is an unceasing fountain bubbling up in the heart; a secret spring the world can't see and doesn't know anything about.

—DWIGHT L. MOODY

37

A cheerful heart is good medicine.

Proverbs 17:22 NIV

A Moment to Refresh

I have set the LORD always before me. Because he is at my right hand, I will not be shaken. Therefore my heart is glad and my tongue rejoices; my body also will rest secure. You have made known to me the path of life; you will fill me with joy in your presence, with eternal pleasures at your right hand.

Psalm 16:8–9, 11 NIV

All the days of those who are crushed are filled with pain and suffering. But a cheerful heart enjoys a good time that never ends.

Proverbs 15:15 NIRV

Jesus said, "I love you just as the Father loves me; remain in my love . . . I have told you this so that my joy may be in you and that your joy may be complete."

John 15:9, 11 GNT

*Wondrous is the strength of cheerfulness, and its power of
endurance—the cheerful man will do more in the same time,
will do it better, and will preserve it longer,
than the sad or sullen.*

—THOMAS CARLYLE

*God's Kingdom is not a matter of eating
and drinking, but of the righteousness,
peace, and joy which the Holy Spirit gives.*
Romans 14:17 GNT

*You love Jesus, although you have not seen
him, and you believe in him, although you
do not now see him. So you rejoice with a
great and glorious joy which words cannot
express, because you are receiving the
salvation of your souls, which is the
purpose of your faith in him.*
1 Peter 1:8–9 GNT

*May God, the source of hope, fill you with
all joy and peace by means of your faith in
him, so that your hope will continue to
grow by the power of the Holy Spirit.*
Romans 15:13 GNT

*Let us be of good
cheer, remembering
that the misfortunes
hardest to bear are
those which
never happen.*

—JAMES RUSSELL
LOWELL

Constant and True

A Moment to Pause

Perhaps today you feel your time has been filled with nothing but a barrage of the rather ordinary—routine e-mails to answer, mundane meetings to attend, customary conversations, and unremarkable encounters. If so, step away for a few moments and reenergize yourself and your day by considering the quality of confidence. Think about where and how you derive your confidence.

Perhaps your personal experience and knowledge provide an important measure of confidence. Perhaps the proven quality and effectiveness of your leadership provides confidence as well. While these components are valid, they are subject to change with time and circumstance.

God offers an internal vote of assurance, a lasting confidence that finds its source in him. True confidence is a position of the soul. It is the quiet repose of the heart that enjoys a secure and trusting relationship with God. It is the calm surety of the mind that rests in knowledge of his truth.

Enduring confidence does not change with the circumstances or the competition, because God, in whom you place your confidence, remains constant and true. In fact, the Bible states that with God there is no variation. He does not change. He is worthy of confidence.

Skill and confidence are an unconquered army.
—*George Herbert*

A Moment to Reflect

You decide to have confidence in another person when you learn about the person's capabilities and dependability. Based on prior performance or demonstrated skills, you choose to believe that person will be equally effective in the future.

Today you can discover enduring confidence by choosing to depend upon God's unchanging nature and upon the truth of his Word. As you read the verses on the next pages, take note of the characteristics of God that merit confidence in him. Also note the many benefits of placing your confidence in the Lord. As these benefits are granted to you, they will advantageously affect those you lead as well.

Sometimes we get unduly elated when things go well, and at other times we are too dejected when they go badly ... What we need is to establish our heart firmly in God's strength, and struggle as best we can to place all our confidence and hope in him.

—JORDAN OF SAXONY

Have no fear of sudden disaster or of the ruin that overtakes the wicked, for the LORD will be your confidence and will keep your foot from being snared.

Proverbs 3:25–26 NIV

A Moment to Refresh

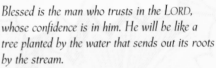

Blessed is the man who trusts in the LORD, whose confidence is in him. He will be like a tree planted by the water that sends out its roots by the stream.

Jeremiah 17:7–8 NIV

Our proud confidence is this: the testimony of our conscience, that in holiness and godly sincerity, not in fleshly wisdom but in the grace of God, we have conducted ourselves in the world, and especially toward you.

2 Corinthians 1:12 NASB

Let us draw near with confidence to the throne of grace, so that we may receive mercy and find grace to help in time of need.

Hebrews 4:16 NASB

Our confidence in Christ does not make us lazy, negligent, or careless, but on the contrary it awakens us, urges us on, and makes us active in living righteous lives and doing good.

—ULRICH ZWINGLI

We know and rely on the love God has for us. God is love. Whoever lives in love lives in God and God in him. In this way, love is made complete among us so that we will have confidence on the day of judgment, because in this world we are like him.
1 John 4:16–17 NIV

In union with Christ and through our faith in him we have the boldness to go into God's presence with all confidence.
Ephesians 3:12 GNT

Do not throw away your confidence, which has a great reward.
Hebrews 10:35 NASB

Dear friends, if our hearts do not condemn us, we have confidence before God.
1 John 3:21 NIV

Faith is a living, daring confidence in God's grace, so sure and certain that a man would stake his life on it a thousand times.

—MARTIN LUTHER

Wonderful Counselor

A Moment to Pause Set aside a few moments to enjoy a time of relaxation apart from observers or intruders. Now consider the people for whom you function as a mentor and counselor. Recall the ways you help them through personal challenges and hurdles. Although your position of leadership allows you to share the wisdom of your experience with others, you may not yourself have the benefit of a relationship with someone who counsels or mentors you. If you had such a person with you now, what would be at the top of your list to discuss?

Each day you feel the weight of responsibility. You recognize the impact of your decisions on the lives of others. You may also feel a deep, inner need for a confidential and wise adviser. Recognize today that God is available to counsel and mentor you, and he offers his Word as a source of insight.

Allowing God to mentor and counsel you through his Word can be of great help in reducing personal stress and in maintaining a clear vision of priorities. He will help you steer your way through daily pressures and trials. He will guide your heart and mind to discover truth and grow in wisdom.

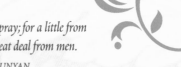

Pray and read, read and pray; for a little from
God is better than a great deal from men.
—JOHN BUNYAN

A Moment to Reflect

Recall the item that would be on the top of your list to discuss with a trusted mentor. Spend a few minutes talking to God about that matter. Then turn to God's Word to receive insight and guidance.

The Bible contains leadership lessons that continue to be relevant today. Note the practices of Old and New Testament leaders that brought them great success in the eyes of others and of God. Observe how Jesus led by example and encouragement. Study the leadership principles within the book of Proverbs. Ask God to be your mentor as he guides you through his Word.

We will never understand the full meaning of Jesus' richly varied ministry unless we see how the many things are rooted in the one thing: listening to the Father in the intimacy of perfect love. When we see this, we will also realize the goal of Jesus' ministry is nothing less than to bring us into this most intimate community.

—Henri J. M. Nouwen

*I will praise the LORD, who counsels me; even
at night my heart instructs me.*

Psalm 16:7 NIV

A Moment to Refresh

*For to us a child is born, to us a son is given,
and the government will be on his shoulders.
And he will be called Wonderful Counselor,
Mighty God, Everlasting Father,
Prince of Peace.*

Isaiah 9:6 NIV

*The law of the LORD is perfect, reviving the
soul. The statutes of the LORD are trustworthy,
making wise the simple . . . The fear of the
LORD is pure, enduring forever. The ordinances
of the LORD are sure and altogether righteous.*

Psalm 19:7, 9 NIV

*The counsel of the Lord stands forever,
The plans of His heart from generation
to generation.*

Psalm 33:11 NASB

When the Bible speaks, God speaks.

—B. B. WARFIELD

I will instruct you and teach you in the way you should go; I will counsel you and watch over you.

Psalm 32:8 NIV

Those who are led by the Spirit of God are children of God.

Romans 8:14 NIRV

Teach me your way, O Lord, and I will walk in your truth; give me an undivided heart, that I may fear your name.

Psalm 86:11 NIV

Jesus said, "When, however, the Spirit comes, who reveals the truth about God, he will lead you into all the truth. He will not speak on his own authority, but he will speak of what he hears and will tell you of things to come. He will give me glory, because he will take what I say and tell it to you."

John 16:13–14 GNT

The secret of my success? It is simple. It is found in the Bible, "In all thy ways acknowledge Him and He shall direct thy paths."

—GEORGE
WASHINGTON CARVER

47

Light in the Darkness

A Moment to Pause

Prepare yourself for a break by putting aside your work. Close your eyes and breathe deeply to help your mind and body relax. As you shut the light away from your eyes, remember the last time you looked into the night sky. Recall the vast darkness of space as it extended outward for inestimable miles.

In much the same way, mounting difficulties and dark questions sometimes stretch ahead as far as you can foresee. Often the details of these challenging situations cannot be revealed to others because of the need to protect business interests or to protect co-workers. Leaders are often called on to face these challenges alone. One important aspect of successful leadership is learning to see the light of possibility, even in times of difficulty.

Just as the glare of the midday sun obscures the distant stars, shining success in business can obscure changes or improvements that are necessary for future productivity. However, just as stars become visible in the midst of darkness, new potentials shine in the midst of challenges.

Darkness is not purposeless. God can use difficult times to bring new options to light. Effective leaders have learned to see the possibilities.

*The stars are constantly shining, but often we
do not see them until the dark hours.*

—EARL RINEY

A Moment to Reflect

Take a new look at the possibilities that surround you today. What opportunities do you have to address unmet needs in your area of service or to adjust to future contingencies? What opportunities do you have to set new standards of performance? Consider those in your organization who have untapped potential, resources, or ideas.

Recognize that challenges and possibilities continually coexist in any organization. Rather than expending the bulk of your time and energy confronting difficulties as the majority of people do, exhibit true leadership by focusing your attention primarily on the possibilities God has afforded you. When in darkness, look for the stars.

Out of deep darkness,
You brought forth your light,
Spangling the heavens
With stars in the night.
So remind me, Lord,
When the darkness surrounds,
Wondrous new treasures
Are there to be found.

ೋ

—MELINDA MAHAND

49

Even in darkness light dawns for the upright,
for the gracious and compassionate and
righteous man.

Psalm 112:4 NIV

A Moment to Refresh

God is light, and in him is no darkness at all.

1 John 1:5 KJV

When Jesus spoke again to the people, he said,
"I am the light of the world. Whoever follows
me will never walk in darkness, but will have
the light of life."

John 8:12 NIV

The God who said, "Out of darkness the light
shall shine!" is the same God who made his
light shine in our hearts, to bring us the
knowledge of God's glory shining in the
face of Christ.

2 Corinthians 4:6 GNT

The LORD is my light and my salvation—whom
shall I fear?

Psalm 27:1 NIV

Live in faith and hope, though it be in darkness, for in this darkness God protects the soul. Cast your care upon God, for you are His and He will not forget you.

—Saint John of the Cross

Our God is tender and caring. His kindness will bring the rising sun to us from heaven. It will shine on those living in darkness and in the shadow of death. It will guide our feet on the path of peace.

Luke 1:78–79 NIRV

You are a chosen people, a royal priesthood, a holy nation, a people belonging to God, that you may declare the praises of him who called you out of darkness into his wonderful light.

1 Peter 2:9 NIV

You were once darkness, but now you are light in the Lord. Live as children of light (for the fruit of the light consists in all goodness, righteousness and truth).

Ephesians 5:8–9 NIV

In darkness there is no choice. It is light that enables us to see the differences between things; and it is Christ who gives us light.

—Augustus W. Hare

51

Good Intentions

A Moment to Pause Reward yourself for a job well done by enjoying a few unhurried moments of solitude. Though as a leader you spend much of your day addressing the needs of others, spend these minutes addressing your own need of renewal. By being good to yourself in this respect, you are actually benefiting all those who look to you for leadership and guidance.

As you begin to unwind, think of the people to whom you have recently extended goodness and grace. Are there people who carried out a task poorly or worked ineffectively and yet received your help and understanding rather than reprisal? This type of gracious goodness is a sign of true leadership. Great leaders grasp such challenges as opportunities to train and coach rather than to punish.

Yet as apt as you may be to forgive others and consider their mistakes as occasions for teaching, you probably may be reluctant to offer that same forbearance to yourself. Leaders are rarely more demanding of others than they are of themselves. After a while, the weight of your own demands and the burden of your own shortcomings become difficult to bear. You, like those you lead, find yourself in need of grace.

We serve a gracious Master who knows how to overrule even our mistakes to His glory and our advantage.
—John Newton

A Moment to Reflect

As you seek to fulfill your calling of leadership, God makes his grace continually available to you. Grace is God's choice to bless you and do good on your behalf. It is not based on your behavior or performance, but on his nature and his will alone. So when you fail or make a mistake, God's gracious nature and will spurs him to do good for you anyway. His gracious goodness uses your trials and mistakes to strengthen and train you.

Decide today to become coachable. Let God's gracious goodness teach you and bless you. Ask for and thankfully expect to see his goodness and his grace.

Amazing grace! how sweet the sound
That saved a wretch like me;
I once was lost, but now I'm found;
Was blind, but now I see.
Thru many dangers, toils, and snares,
I have already come;
'Tis grace hath brought me safe thus far;
And grace will lead me home.

—John Newton

The LORD is good to those whose hope is in him, to the one who seeks him; it is good to wait quietly for the salvation of the LORD.

Lamentations 3:25–26 NIV

A Moment to Refresh

How great is your goodness, which you have stored up for those who fear you, which you bestow in the sight of men on those who take refuge in you.

Psalm 31:19 NIV

Since ancient times no one has heard, no ear has perceived, no eye has seen any God besides you, who acts on behalf of those who wait for him. You come to the help of those who gladly do right, who remember your ways.

Isaiah 64:4–5 NIV

God is able to make all grace abound to you, so that in all things at all times, having all that you need, you will abound in every good work.

2 Corinthians 9:8 NIV

Your worst days are never so bad that you are beyond the reach
of God's grace. And your best days are never so good that you
are beyond the need of God's grace.

—JERRY BRIDGES

The LORD is gracious and compassionate,
slow to anger and rich in love. The LORD
is good to all; he has compassion on all he
has made.

Psalm 145:8–9 NIV

Praise the LORD. Give thanks to the LORD,
for he is good; his love endures forever.

Psalm 106:1 NIV

From the fullness of his grace we have all
received one blessing after another.

John 1:16 NIV

The LORD is good and his love endures
forever; his faithfulness continues through
all generations.

Psalm 100:5 NIV

Grace is love that
cares and stoops
and rescues.

—JOHN STOTT

An Arm of Strength

A Moment to Pause Go outdoors for today's retreat, or close the door to your office and look outside the window. Take note of aspects of nature that catch your eye and demonstrate God's strength—the sun, the rain, the sturdy trees, the fragrant flowers, the flowing river, the trickling stream. Spend these minutes refocusing on God and considering the strength he has to offer you.

You continually expend your energy by giving an arm of strength to those around you. You give strength to encourage and support others. You give strength to motivate and activate others. No wonder you often come to the end of your day feeling like you are given out.

Yet just as you, in your position as a leader, offer your strength to others, so God, in his omnipotence, offers you his arm of strength. In times when you feel weak, God can supply you with an inexhaustible source of strength. He will infuse your life and work with his power.

Your expenditure of strength and energy then becomes much like that of a weight trainer or bodybuilder. When accompanied by proper attention to your physical need for rest and nourishment, today's workout tones and prepares you, making you better able to meet the challenge of tomorrow.

Rest on God. His arm, not your own, must be
your strength. Fear God and no other fear
shall ever trouble you.

—Joseph Parker

A Moment to Reflect **G**od knows your leadership task requires strength, but it is God's strength—not yours alone—that will make your work effective and give it impact. God is the power that recharges your soul and gives you the strength to continue.

Spend time considering the verses on the following pages. Through prayer and faith, claim their power for your leadership. Recognize the privilege God affords you when he provides his strength to work in and through you. In his strength, you can accomplish his purposes on this earth. Feel the honor and experience the anticipation of his strength in you.

When God wants to move a mountain, he does not take a bar of iron, but he takes a little worm. The fact is, we have too much strength. We are not weak enough. It is not our strength that we want. One drop of God's strength is worth more than all the world.

୬

—DWIGHT L. MOODY

Do not fear, for I am with you; do not be dismayed, for I am your God. I will strengthen you and help you; I will uphold you with my righteous right hand.

Isaiah 41:10 NIV

A Moment to Refresh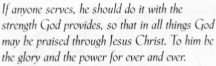

If anyone serves, he should do it with the strength God provides, so that in all things God may be praised through Jesus Christ. To him be the glory and the power for ever and ever.

1 Peter 4:11 NIV

God gives strength to the weary and increases the power of the weak.

Isaiah 40:29 NIV

May our Lord Jesus Christ himself and God our Father, who loved us and by his grace gave us eternal encouragement and good hope, encourage your hearts and strengthen you in every good deed and word.

2 Thessalonians 2:16–17 NIV

A man who is intimate with God will never be intimidated by men.

ᘐ

—LEONARD RAVENHILL

O LORD God Almighty, who is like you?
You are mighty, O LORD, and your
faithfulness surrounds you. Your arm is
endued with power; your hand is strong,
your right hand exalted.

Psalm 89:8, 13 NIV

The LORD and King is coming with power.
His powerful arm will rule for him. He has
set his people free. He is bringing them
back as his reward. He has won the battle
over their enemies.

Isaiah 40:10 NIRV

The eternal God is your refuge, and
underneath are the everlasting arms.

Deuteronomy 33:27 NIV

When a man has no
strength, if he leans
on God, he becomes
powerful.

ᘐ

—DWIGHT L. MOODY

Picking up the Pieces

A Moment to Pause   If projects and goals seem to be off course and crumbling before you, take this opportunity to begin picking up the pieces. Close your door and claim a few private minutes with God. Although you know your organization's projections and plans, God knows the final outcomes. You need to talk to him.

The Bible contains example after example of leaders who turned to God in times of difficulty. They told him their fears, and they told him their aspirations. One by one, God responded to their prayers by acting mightily on their behalf. He responded with wondrous deeds.

Today you, too, have access to God, just as did the leaders of long ago. Prayer is your direct line of communication with the One who has ultimate authority in heaven and on earth. Prayer can ease your stress, provide you with guidance, give you confidence, and increase your productivity.

Recognize that there is an ear ready to listen and a hand ready to move on your behalf today. He will help you pick up the pieces. He may even help you put them together again. Or God may have something else in store for you—he may choose to begin a new work in you altogether.

Prayer moves the hand that moves the world.

—AUTHOR UNKNOWN

A Moment to Reflect

Scripture states that prayer results in a wide variety of benefits: peace, power, wisdom, and assurance, to name a few. No one has ever seen the limit of what God will do for the person who turns to him in prayer.

This very moment is an occasion to expect great things from God. Consider the opportunities you have had as a leader that you never actually asked for. Consider the many blessings you have enjoyed in life that you never even sought. What else might God be planning for you if you only request it of him today? It would be worth finding out.

Each time, before you intercede, be quiet first, and worship God in His glory. Think of what He can do, and how He delights to hear the prayers of His redeemed people. Think of your place and privilege in Christ, and expect great things!

—ANDREW MURRAY

Whenever you pray, go into your room and shut the door and pray to your Father who is in secret; and your Father who sees in secret will reward you.

Matthew 6:6 NRSV

A Moment to Refresh

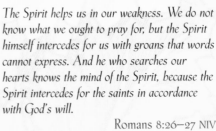

The Spirit helps us in our weakness. We do not know what we ought to pray for, but the Spirit himself intercedes for us with groans that words cannot express. And he who searches our hearts knows the mind of the Spirit, because the Spirit intercedes for the saints in accordance with God's will.

Romans 8:26–27 NIV

The LORD is far from the wicked but he hears the prayer of the righteous.

Proverbs 15:29 NIV

The prayer of a righteous man is powerful and effective.

James 5:16 NIV

The eyes of the Lord are on the righteous and his ears are attentive to their prayer.

1 Peter 3:10 NIV

One of the best ways to get on your feet is to first get on your knees.

—AUTHOR UNKNOWN

Be clear minded and self-controlled so that you can pray.

1 Peter 4:7 NIV

Whatever you ask for in prayer, believe that you have received it, and it will be yours.

Mark 11:24 NRSV

Give ear to my words, O LORD, consider my sighing. Listen to my cry for help, my King and my God, for to you I pray. In the morning, O LORD, you hear my voice; in the morning I lay my requests before you and wait in expectation.

Psalm 5:1–3 NIV

The LORD detests the sacrifice of the wicked, but the prayer of the upright pleases him.

Proverbs 15:8 NIV

Prayer is my chief work, by it I carry on all else.

—WILLIAM LAW

63

When the Going Gets Tough

A Moment to Pause

Appropriating a few minutes to focus your thoughts and energize your soul can be tough sometimes for a leader, but the results are worth the extra effort. Stop now and enjoy a few moments of relaxation. Close your eyes and remember a time when you have floated on the water, whether on a raft in a pool, in a canoe on a stream, or on your back atop gentle ocean waves. Recall the peace of that moment, and let that peace calm your spirit once again.

Water, however, has another characteristic besides its ability to bring tranquility. It can also prove to be a powerful force. Imagine, for instance, a rushing mountain brook with large boulders along the way. At first glance, the water seems to give way to the boulder, diverting to another path. Yet something more is happening. The water is not only finding another path for the present, it is eroding the barrier to its progress and clearing the path for the future. Leaders operate in much the same way.

Obstacles of time, budgeting, and staffing often loom in your path, making progress tough. Your challenge is to prevent such obstacles from bringing work to a standstill. To meet this challenge, you must employ determination and use efficiency and ingenuity to move steadily forward.

Leaders are ordinary people with
extraordinary determination.
—AUTHOR UNKNOWN

A Moment to Reflect

Determination is remaining committed to the goal, even when it isn't easy and even when it costs you. Many people may have what it takes to get a project up and running, but it takes a leader to maintain the determination, stay the course, and see the project through to completion. Keep striving until you obtain success.

Identify the most challenging task you currently face. Ask God to renew your determination and fill you with his strength. Then focus your energy toward successfully attaining your goal. In the end, your determination will prevail and your vision will be realized.

We are undefeated as long as we keep on trying, as long as we have some source of movement within ourselves and are not just moved by outside forces, as long as we retain the freedom of right decision and action, whatever the circumstances.

—George Appleton

Though a righteous man falls seven times,
he rises again.

Proverbs 24:16 NIV

A Moment to Refresh

As for me, I watch in hope for the LORD, I wait for God my Savior; my God will hear me. Do not gloat over me, my enemy! Though I have fallen, I will rise. Though I sit in darkness, the LORD will be my light.

Micah 7:7–8 NIV

We who have this spiritual treasure are like common clay pots, in order to show that the supreme power belongs to God, not to us. We are often troubled, but not crushed; sometimes in doubt, but never in despair; there are many enemies, but we are never without a friend; and though badly hurt at times, we are not destroyed . . . For this reason we never become discouraged. Even though our physical being is gradually decaying, yet our spiritual being is renewed day after day.

2 Corinthians 4:7–9, 16 GNT

Success is often a matter of holding on after others have let go.

—JOHN L. MASON

*If the LORD delights in a man's way, he
makes his steps firm; though he stumble, he
will not fall, for the LORD upholds him with
his hand.*

Psalm 37:23–24 NIV

By your endurance you will gain your lives.

Luke 21:19 NASB

*The LORD upholds all those who fall and
lifts up all who are bowed down.*

Psalm 145:14 NIV

*The Lord said, "My power is made perfect
in weakness."*

2 Corinthians 12:9 NIV

*It is God who works in you to will and to
act according to his good purpose.*

Philippians 2:13 NIV

*Never forget that
only dead fish swim
with the stream.*

—MALCOLM
MUGGERIDGE

When God Chooses

A Moment to Pause Lean back and take several slow, deep breaths. Notice that breathing at a slower pace has a relaxing influence on your body. As a leader, you know the importance of timing. Just as slowing the pace of your breathing affects your body, so does slowing the pace of your life and waiting on God's timing to affect your soul.

Because of your drive to clear new pathways and instigate change, it would be easy to forget to wait for the timing of God in some endeavors. If today you find yourself struggling to submit your plan to God's timing, take a moment to enjoy and learn from the following short parable:

Long ago a simple farmer was carrying a crate of eggs to market. As he walked, he started calculating how much money he would receive for the day's yield. When he had that figure, he next planned what to purchase with the income and how to resell his purchases at a profit.

Soon he was imagining glorious possibilities of multiplied returns, and he reveled in the luxuries he could then afford. Yet as he envisioned this prosperous future, he lost sight of the task at hand. He stumbled over a stone on the path, fell down face first, and broke the eggs.

Not only in his will, but in the season appointed
by his will, is our peace. My hour will come,
when it is his hour.
—William Quinlan Lash

A Moment to Reflect

*I*n his eagerness to secure a successful future, the farmer forgot the task at hand and landed facedown in the dirt. Guard that you, as a leader, keep focused on where you are going and how you are going to get there so that you don't stumble before reaching your goal. Humility provides the answer to this tendency.

Humility will guide you to stay in touch with your company's day-to-day operations because success demands that you keep your feet firmly planted in today. Humility will remind you to show gratitude, and humility will protect you from landing in the dirt because it is the humble leader whom God exalts—in his own time.

I used to think that God's gifts were on shelves one above the other and that the taller we grew in Christian character the more easily we could reach them. I now find that God's gifts are on shelves one beneath the other and that it is not a question of growing taller but of stooping lower.

—F. B. MEYER

*All who exalt themselves will be humbled, and
those who humble themselves will be exalted.*

Luke 14:11 NRSV

A Moment to Refresh

*The fear of the LORD teaches a man wisdom,
and humility comes before honor.*

Proverbs 15:33 NIV

*At the proper time we will reap a harvest if we
do not give up.*

Galatians 6:9 NIV

*Clothe yourselves with humility toward one
another, because, "God opposes the proud but
gives grace to the humble." Humble yourselves,
therefore, under God's mighty hand, that he
may lift you up in due time.*

1 Peter 5:5–6 NIV

*A man's pride will bring him low, but a humble
spirit will obtain honor.*

Proverbs 29:23 NASB

It took me years to learn that God has a timing all His own and that I must not be impatient when His timing doesn't coincide with mine.

—David Wilkerson

Humble yourselves before the Lord, and he will lift you up.

James 4:10 NIV

Humility and the fear of the LORD bring wealth and honor and life.

Proverbs 22:4 NIV

The humble will inherit the land, and will delight themselves in abundant prosperity.

Psalm 37:11 NASB

Trust in the LORD and do good. Then you will live safely in the land and prosper. Take delight in the LORD, and he will give you your heart's desires.

Psalm 37:3–4 NIV

Certain things are not refused us, but their granting is delayed to a fitting time.

—Saint Augustine of Hippo

True Leadership

A Moment to Pause

Retreat today to a place of quietness such as a nearby park, an outdoor fountain, or a local chapel. Choose a place where you can pause to become aware of God's presence with you. Ask him to help you recognize the ways you have demonstrated effective leadership today, realizing that leadership is more than simply telling others what to do. Leadership is showing others how to develop and advance.

The true greatness of a leader is measured not only in profit margins and market share, but also in ultimate influence. And although you may not be aware of it on a daily basis, your influence reaches far beyond your present peers, employees, and business contacts.

Just as the influence of the moon draws waves to the shore and, in so doing, affects the lives of the creatures living within the water's tow, your influence affects not only your co-workers and subordinates, but it also affects those with whom your co-workers and subordinates come in contact. Just as energy and matter never dissipate but simply change from form to form, so your influence does not die. It simply transfers from one life to another, investing itself over and over again.

One of the marks of true greatness is the ability
to develop greatness in others.
—J. C. MACAULAY

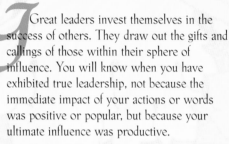

A Moment to Reflect

Great leaders invest themselves in the success of others. They draw out the gifts and callings of those within their sphere of influence. You will know when you have exhibited true leadership, not because the immediate impact of your actions or words was positive or popular, but because your ultimate influence was productive.

Such influence makes it possible for you to be an instrument of God in others' lives. Ask him today to so influence your mind and heart that you become a clear example of his truth. May your influence ultimately lead others not merely to become like you, but to become more like him.

You are not a great leader simply because others follow your commands. One who merely issues commands has denigrated himself to the level of taskmaster. Instead, you are a great leader when others follow your character. Leaders mold and shape and fashion character. Leaders take part in the very activity of God, for they create others in their own likeness.

—MELINDA MAHAND

The righteous man is a guide to his friend.
Proverbs 12:26 GNT

A Moment to Refresh

The path of the righteous is like the first gleam
of dawn, shining ever brighter until the full
light of day.

Proverbs 4:18 NIV

Jesus said, "I have set you an example that you
should do as I have done for you."

John 13:15 NIV

Think of yourself with sober judgment, in
accordance with the measure of faith God has
given you. Just as each of us has one body with
many members, and these members do not all
have the same function, so in Christ we who are
many form one body, and each member belongs
to all the others. If a man's gift is . . .
leadership, let him govern diligently.

Romans 12:3–6, 8 NIV

We are all leaders, or potential leaders. We are all required to be prepared to receive a leading, or a prompting which may call us and others in directions we had not dreamt of.

—MARGARET HEATHFIELD

A student is not above his teacher, but everyone who is fully trained will be like his teacher.

Luke 6:40 NIV

Remember your leaders, who spoke the word of God to you. Consider the outcome of their way of life and imitate their faith.

Hebrews 13:7 NIV

We desire that each one of you show the same diligence so as to realize the full assurance of hope until the end, that you may not be sluggish, but imitators of those who through faith and patience inherit the promises.

Hebrews 6:11–12 NASB

The greatest power for good is the power of example.

—AUTHOR
UNKNOWN

Access Offered

A Moment to Pause Step away from the serious concerns of leadership and enjoy a moment of trivia. See if you can answer this fun question: Why are your last set of molars called wisdom teeth? Answer? Because wisdom teeth are the last to erupt.

Permanent teeth begin to erupt when a child is six years old, but wisdom teeth don't erupt until a person is in his late teens or early twenties. People in previous centuries believed the cutting of these teeth was a sign that an individual had attained maturity and discretion, that is, that they had attained wisdom. Individuals were not allowed to assume positions of leadership until the wisdom teeth emerged.

Today people no longer believe they can access wisdom by cutting a few molars, but some continue to think they can access wisdom by growing older. Others believe wisdom comes when they acquire prodigious knowledge, advanced degrees, or certain life experiences. Each of these beliefs, however, is as much a misperception as the ancient outlook regarding teeth.

Wisdom is essential for leadership. God says wisdom is more valuable than silver or gold and more precious than rubies. He promises wisdom will bring long life, peace, honor, and riches to the person who possesses it.

You can't access wisdom by the megabyte.
Wisdom is concerned with how we relate to
people, to the world, and to God.
—EDMUND P. CLOWNEY

A Moment to Reflect

The Bible explains that in order to access wisdom, you must spend time with God, immersing yourself in prayer and his Word. As you come into God's presence, ask him to impart wisdom directly to you.

Leadership responsibilities require great wisdom in dealing with business relationships and business endeavors. As a leader, you need wisdom as you make the decisions required of you every day. Reading the verses on the following pages or reading from the book of Proverbs in the Bible is a good way to begin. As you read, ask God to develop his wisdom in you.

Wisdom is the right use of knowledge. To know is not to be wise. There is no fool so great as a knowing fool. But to know how to use knowledge is to have wisdom.

—CHARLES H. SPURGEON

77

*Surely you desire truth in the inner parts; you
teach me wisdom in the inmost place.*

Psalm 51:6 NIV

A Moment to Refresh

*The fear of the LORD is the beginning of
wisdom; all who follow his precepts have good
understanding.*

Psalm 111:10 NIV

*A wise man will hear and increase in learning,
and a man of understanding will acquire wise
counsel.*

Proverbs 1:5 NASB

*Wisdom is better than folly, just as light is
better than darkness.*

Ecclesiastes 2:13 NIV

*If any of you lacks wisdom, he should ask God,
who gives generously to all without finding fault,
and it will be given to him.*

James 1:5 NIV

Wisdom is the ability to use knowledge so as to meet successfully the emergencies of life. Men may acquire knowledge, but wisdom is a gift direct from God.

—Bob Jones

Wisdom is supreme; therefore get wisdom. Though it cost all you have, get understanding. Esteem her, and she will exalt you; embrace her, and she will honor you. She will set a garland of grace on your head and present you with a crown of splendor.

Proverbs 4:7–9 NIV

Blessed is the man who finds wisdom, the man who gains understanding, for she is more profitable than silver and yields better returns than gold. She is more precious than rubies; nothing you desire can compare with her. Long life is in her right hand; in her left hand are riches and honor. Her ways are pleasant ways, and all her paths are peace. She is a tree of life to those who embrace her; those who lay hold of her will be blessed.

Proverbs 3:13–18 NIV

The intellect of the wise is like glass; it admits the light of heaven and reflects it.

—Augustus W. Hare

79

An Unexpected Power

A Moment to Pause

Find a time and place to be alone with God, perhaps as you sit in your car ready to go home at the end of the day. Meditate on the times God has given you strength in your life, and draw new strength from that memory. Now meditate on the times he has given you gentleness, and draw renewed peace from that experience. Although strength and gentleness seem to be diametrically opposed and are not usually considered in conjunction with each other, the reality is that in order to truly deserve the description gentle, a thing—or a leader—must first be strong.

Consider the example of a lion with his cub. When the cub playfully cuffs its father without doing harm, people call the cub weak. Yet when the adult lion playfully cuffs the cub without doing harm, people call the father gentle. Only the strong can be gentle.

The Bible describes God as being all-powerful as well as gentle. God is gentle simply because he has chosen to be, for gentleness is a choice made by the strong when it is in their power to behave instead with harshness or severity or force or cruelty. Few things on earth require more strength than the choice to conduct oneself with gentleness.

Gentle words are hard to despise,
gentle deeds to defeat.
—MELINDA MAHAND

A Moment to Reflect

*K*nowing first that great strength is a prerequisite for gentleness, it becomes easier to understand why gentle words and actions are so powerful, almost irresistibly so. For instance, Proverbs 15:1 advises that a gentle answer turns away wrath. Like the powerful ocean tide, gentleness moves people's hearts and minds without their being conscious of how or when their position changed.

Think of someone within the sphere of your leadership who has resisted authority. Consider trying gentleness with that person. That approach may reach the person more effectively than anger or force. Plan now the gentle words or actions with which you will approach this person.

We have only to spend a day with you, and to see you under trying circumstances, to know your quality. What are gentlefolks? Just what the name implies—gentle, patient, large-minded, large-hearted; not impetuous, fierce, cruel, vengeful, but filled with the spirit of gentleness, taking the kindliest view of every action and every deed, and the happiest when doing most to increase the happiness of others.

—JOSEPH PARKER

Through patience a ruler can be persuaded,
and a gentle tongue can break a bone.

Proverbs 25:15 NIV

A Moment to Refresh

Blessed are the gentle, for they shall inherit
the earth.

Matthew 5:5 NASB

Who is God but the LORD? And who is a
rock, except our God, the God who girds me
with strength And makes my way blameless?
You have also given me the shield of Your
salvation, and Your right hand upholds me; and
Your gentleness makes me great.

Psalm 18:31–32, 35 NASB

Jesus said, "Take my yoke upon you and learn
from me, for I am gentle and humble in heart,
and you will find rest for your souls."

Matthew 11:29 NIV

The fruit of the Spirit is love, joy, peace,
patience, kindness, goodness, faithfulness,
gentleness and self-control. Against such things
there is no law.

Galatians 5:22–23 NIV

Acts of angry violence impact this world, but acts of gentleness impact eternity.

—MELINDA MAHAND

Let your gentleness be evident to all. The Lord is near.

Philippians 4:5 NIV

The wisdom from above is first pure, then peaceable, gentle, reasonable, full of mercy and good fruits, unwavering, without hypocrisy. And the seed whose fruit is righteousness is sown in peace by those who make peace.

James 3:17–18 NASB

As the Lord's servant, you must not quarrel. You must be kind toward all, a good and patient teacher, who is gentle as you correct your opponents, for it may be that God will give them the opportunity to repent and come to know the truth.

2 Timothy 2:24–25 GNT

Nothing is so strong as gentleness; nothing so gentle as real strength.

—SAINT FRANCIS DE SALES

The Door to Success

Lay aside the tasks of the day and allow yourself this brief time of retreat. As you close the door of your office, close your mind to thoughts of people and tasks waiting for your attention. Focus on God and on the success with which he has blessed you. Thank him for the many doors that are open to you as a leader. Most likely, your position gives you access to doors of opportunity and influence that may be closed to most.

These doors are a natural benefit of having already stepped through the door to success. Yet as a leader, you have already learned there is no key that effortlessly turns the lock and opens that door. Whether you imagine that door with a sign that says PUSH or a sign that says PULL, the door to success requires real effort. It requires hard work.

Likewise, people sometimes make the mistake of thinking the Christian life requires no effort on their part. Although God provides a relationship with him as a free gift to those who believe in Jesus, when God describes the type of leader who is a success in his kingdom, God depicts a person who engages in hard work.

Ideas won't work unless you do.
—Author Unknown

A Moment to Reflect

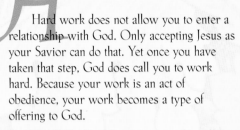

Hard work does not allow you to enter a relationship with God. Only accepting Jesus as your Savior can do that. Yet once you have taken that step, God does call you to work hard. Because your work is an act of obedience, your work becomes a type of offering to God.

The Bible describes a variety of benefits that God supplies as a reward for your work. As you read the verses on the following pages, take note of these benefits. Recognize also that your offering of work, and the benefits God supplies as a result of it, become a testimony of God's power and grace to those who do not yet know him.

Work is the natural exercise and function of man. Work is not primarily a thing one does to live, but the thing one lives to do. It is, or should be, the full expression of the worker's faculties, the thing in which he finds spiritual, mental, and bodily satisfaction, and the medium in which he offers himself to God.

᠀

—Dorothy Leigh Sayers

Whatever your hand finds to do, do it with all your might.

Ecclesiastes 9:10 NIV

A Moment to Refresh

Whatever you do, work at it with all your heart, as working for the Lord, not for men, since you know that you will receive an inheritance from the Lord as a reward. It is the Lord Christ you are serving.

Colossians 3:23–24 NIV

God "will give to each person in keeping with what he has done." God will give eternal life to those who keep on doing good. They want glory, honor, and life that never ends.

Romans 2:6–7 NIRV

Sow your seed in the morning, and at evening do not let your hands be idle, for you do not know which will succeed, whether this or that, or whether both will do equally well.

Ecclesiastes 11:6 NIV

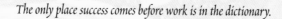

The only place success comes before work is in the dictionary.

—AUTHOR UNKNOWN

Do you see a man skilled at his work? He will serve before kings; he will not serve before obscure men.

Proverbs 22:29 NIV

Let your light shine before men in such as way that they may see your good works, and glorify your Father who is in heaven.

Matthew 5:16 NASB

Do everything without complaining or arguing, so that you may become blameless and pure, children of God without fault in a crooked and depraved generation, in which you shine like stars in the universe as you hold out the word of life.

Philippians 2:14–16 NIV

Steadfast love belongs to you, O Lord, For you repay to all according to their work.

Psalm 62:12 NSRV

If you want your dreams to come true, don't oversleep.

—AUTHOR UNKNOWN

Training for the Task

A Moment to Pause

Leave the demands of your office and find a quiet place to be alone. Begin to release stress from your body by massaging the pressure point in the center of your palm. Firmly massage down the sides of each finger. End by massaging the fleshy area between your thumb and index finger. Rubbing out the knots in this area can help release tension in your shoulders, neck, and back as well.

While massaging, think about the variety of skills for which your hands are disciplined. They can probably keyboard, use a cell phone, operate a remote control, and give visual encouragement or direction without you having to consciously think about those tasks. Through repeated training and discipline, your hands have mastered a variety of skills.

Leaders must likewise seek discipline in other areas of life—the discipline to focus on priorities, to stay on task, to hone your mind and skills to meet not only the challenges of today, but the challenges of tomorrow as well. Just as an athlete works out, trains, and practices all week in order to be ready for the weekend game, you must continually prepare so that when your organization's next great opportunity comes, you are ready to grasp it.

Christian leadership appears to break down into five main ingredients—clear vision, hard work, dogged perseverance, humble service, and iron discipline.
—JOHN STOTT

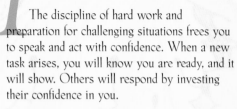

A Moment to Reflect The discipline of hard work and preparation for challenging situations frees you to speak and act with confidence. When a new task arises, you will know you are ready, and it will show. Others will respond by investing their confidence in you.

Yet discipline does not end with preparation. You must make the hard choices and take the daring actions to carry your plans to completion. Once you take on a new task, discipline is the inner grit and steel that gets the job done. Ask God to help you infuse discipline into your strategy for achievement in those areas. Apply discipline in your work, speech, mind-set, and behavior.

No horse gets anywhere until he is harnessed.
No steam or gas ever drives anything until it is
confined. No Niagara is ever turned into light
and power until it is tunneled. No life ever
grows great until it is focused,
dedicated, disciplined.

&

—*HARRY EMERSON FOSDICK*

*He who ignores discipline despises himself, but
whoever heeds correction gains understanding.*
Proverbs 15:32 NIV

A Moment to Refresh

*Our fathers disciplined us for a little while as
they thought best; but God disciplines us for
our good, that we may share in his holiness. No
discipline seems pleasant at the time, but
painful. Later on, however, it produces a harvest
of righteousness and peace for those who have
been trained by it.*

Hebrews 12:10–11 NIV

*The LORD trains those he loves. He is like a
father who trains the son he is pleased with.*
Proverbs 3:12 NIRV

*God has breathed life into all of Scripture. It is
useful for teaching us what is true. It is useful
for correcting our mistakes. It is useful for
making our lives whole again. It is useful for
training us to do what is right. By using
Scripture, a man of God can be completely
prepared to do every good thing.*
2 Timothy 3:16–17 NIRV

God does not discipline us to subdue us, but to condition us for a life of usefulness and blessedness.

—BILLY GRAHAM

God did not give us a spirit of timidity, but a spirit of power, of love and of self-discipline.

2 Timothy 1:7 NIV

He who ignores discipline comes to poverty and shame, but whoever heeds correction is honored.

Proverbs 13:18 NIV

Blessed is the man you discipline, O LORD, the man you teach from your law; you grant him relief from days of trouble.

Psalm 94:12–13 NIV

Watch the path of your feet, and all your ways will be established.

Proverbs 4:26 NASB

A small but always persistent discipline is a great force; for a soft drop falling persistently hollows out hard rock.

—ISAAC FROM SYRIA

Look to the Outcome

A Moment to Pause

Lean back with your arms relaxed at your side. Now close your eyes and breathe deeply and slowly for a moment. If you cannot take an actual power nap, at least claim a power minute. If you face adversity today, a moment of peace to help you keep the day's challenges in proper perspective becomes crucial. When the heat goes up, a leader's temperature must come down.

Your position of leadership requires that you stay cool and calm in the face of adversity. For the good of those who look to you as well as for the good of the organization, it is essential that you remain a source of optimism and hope. The secret of maintaining a calm and confident attitude and approach is the ability to see past the immediate circumstances to what lies beyond.

In many ways, a leader is like a jeweler. To the untrained eye, precious stones tumbling in a polisher seem to be experiencing adverse conditions. But a jeweler understands the stones must go through this period of polishing and shaping in order to become gems. Likewise, a leader knows that adverse conditions can serve to polish and shape people as well as organizations.

Troubles are often the tools by which God fashions us for better things.
—*HENRY WARD BEECHER*

A Moment to Reflect

The true test of your leadership ability arrives at the same moment adversity does. A true leader does not automatically view adversity as a bad thing; he knows that adversity can inspire a new solution. A leader partners with God to see beyond the adversity to the potential outcome.

Let the adversity arouse your competitive spirit so you can think clearly and quickly, and act decisively. Sort out the details, set your priorities, make a decision, or do what you can to find the solution. Then take action to ensure that a similar problem does not occur again. Adversity is your opportunity to do combat and win.

A smooth sea never made a skillful mariner,
neither do uninterrupted prosperity and success
qualify for usefulness and happiness. The storms
of adversity, like those of the ocean, rouse the
faculties, and excite the invention, prudence, skill
and fortitude of the voyager.

—Author Unknown

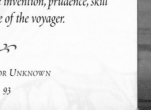

93

*A righteous man may have many troubles, but
the L*ORD *delivers him from them all.*

Psalm 34:19 NIV

A Moment to Refresh

*Our troubles are small. They last only for a
short time. But they are earning for us a glory
that will last forever. It is greater than all our
troubles.*

2 Corinthians 4:17 NIRV

*May those who sow in tears reap with shouts
of joy.*

Psalm 126:5 NSRV

*Cast your cares on the L*ORD *and he will
sustain you; he will never let the righteous fall.*

Psalm 55:22 NIV

*Dear friends, do not be surprised at the painful
trial you are suffering, as though something
strange were happening to you. But rejoice that
you participate in the sufferings of Christ, so
that you may be overjoyed when his glory is
revealed.*

1 Peter 4:12–13 NIV

Fire is the test of gold; adversity, of strong men.

—*Seneca*

Cast all your anxiety on him because he cares for you.

1 Peter 5:7 NIV

You have joy even though you may have had to suffer for a little while. You may have had to suffer sadness in all kinds of trouble. Your troubles have come in order to prove that your faith is real. It is worth more than gold. Gold can pass away even though fire has made it pure. Your faith is meant to bring praise, honor and glory to God. That will happen when Jesus returns.

1 Peter 1:6–7 NIRV

The LORD said, "He will call upon me, and I will answer him; I will be with him in trouble, I will deliver him and honor him."

Psalm 91:15 NIV

At the timberline where the storms strike with the most fury, the sturdiest trees are found.

—*Hudson Taylor*

What Do You Know?

A Moment to Pause Carve out a time today to escape the flurry of appointments, e-mails, messages, and requests. Spend these moments renewing communication with God. Walking to an atrium area or looking through a window might help you focus on him. Even though knowing God is personal, it has a profound effect on your role as a leader. All knowledge affects your leadership, because your knowledge—and the actions you take and decisions you make because of that knowledge—is integral to who you are.

Knowledge is power. You are continually challenged to know your industry, its components, and its competitors. You need to know the people who are powerful and influential and on the cutting edge of your industry. You must watch the trends and anticipate the next great breakthrough.

Today's leaders are presented with an additional challenge. For centuries, knowledge in a particular field stayed relatively the same throughout life. Now, however, in this high-tech society, what is known is soon surpassed, often in the same day. Leaders must update their knowledge day by day and sometimes moment by moment.

Find stability in this world of flux with the assurance that God is the same yesterday, today, and forever. He is your mainstay and anchor. He will keep you grounded in this world of change.

There is but one thing in the world really worth
pursuing—the knowledge of God.
—ROBERT HUGH BENSON

A Moment to Reflect

A leader who seeks to know God and gains his sense of purpose from that relationship has great capacity for inspiration and creativity in all endeavors. He is a person of focus who sees only the purpose and hears only the calling. His ear is not tuned to objection and his eye is not distracted by obstacle or disturbed by change.

Knowledge of and focus on a single purpose is the key to success. Clear understanding of purpose economizes time and enables strength. Focus on the one thing you know that God has called and purposed you to do. This will provide context and meaning for all the other details.

Eternal God, the light of the minds that know you, the joy of the hearts that love you and the strength of the wills that serve you; grant us so to know you, that we may truly love you, and so to love you that we may fully serve you, whom to serve is perfect freedom.

—SAINT AUGUSTINE OF HIPPO

97

*I know whom I have believed and I am
convinced that He is able to guard what I have
entrusted to Him until that day.*

2 Timothy 1:12 NASB

A Moment to Refresh

*Grow in the grace and knowledge of our Lord
and Savior Jesus Christ. To him be glory both
now and forever!*

2 Peter 3:18 NIV

*We have always prayed for you, ever since we
heard about you. We ask God to fill you with
the knowledge of his will, with all the wisdom
and understanding that his Spirit gives. Then
you will be able to live as the Lord wants and
will always do what pleases him. Your lives will
produce all kinds of good deeds, and you will
grow in our knowledge of God.*

Colossians 1:9–10 GNT

*Grace and peace be yours in abundance through
the knowledge of God and of Jesus our Lord.
His divine power has given us everything we
need for life and godliness through our
knowledge of him who called us by his own
glory and goodness.*

2 Peter 1:2–3 NIV

What is the best thing in life? To know God.

—J. I. PACKER

This is eternal life: that they may know you, the only true God, and Jesus Christ, whom you have sent.

John 17:3 NIV

Be still, and know that I am God; I will be exalted among the nations, I will be exalted in the earth.

Psalm 46:10 NIV

I pray that you, being rooted and established in love, may have power, together with all the saints, to grasp how wide and long and high and deep is the love of Christ, and to know this love that surpasses knowledge—that you may be filled to the measure of all the fullness of God.

Ephesians 3:17–19 NIV

Oh, the fullness, pleasure, sheer excitement of knowing God on Earth!

—JIM ELLIOT

Never Alone

A Moment to Pause

While many people may seek time with you today, God is waiting for that one-on-one time as well. If possible, find a place free of noise and other distractions. Settle into a comfortable position and ask God to direct your thoughts as you spend the next few moments focusing on him. These moments may refresh your mind and soul. They should also remind you that you are never alone. God is with you every moment of every day. In fact, one of the attributes that distinguishes God as God rather than as creature is his omnipresence. He is in all places at all times.

Just being in an endeavor with other leaders and achievers gives you confidence. If you are asked to put your name, time, or money behind a new venture, one of the first things you want to know is, who else is in it with you. Likewise, you should draw confidence from the knowledge that God is with you in all your endeavors.

God is not there simply as an observer or companion. He is there to strengthen, help, and guide you. His direction will never be a misjudgment because just as he is ever-present, he is also all-knowing. Nothing that occurs today will surprise him. Nothing that occurs tomorrow will catch him off guard.

God is always near you and with you;
leave him not alone.
—BROTHER LAWRENCE

A Moment to Reflect

Developing a continual awareness of God's presence takes practice, but the confidence and sense of security it brings is worth the effort. Place visual reminders of his presence in strategic places to encourage you throughout the day. For instance, you might print the scripture selections for this retreat on separate index cards. Place one in your car, one in your desk drawer, and one by your nightstand at home.

Each time you see one of the verses, consciously choose to believe the claim the verse makes. Take just a moment to refocus and acknowledge God's presence with you. By becoming aware of his presence, you will begin to experience his power as well.

One of the most powerful concepts, one which is a sure cure for lack of confidence, is the thought that God is with you and helping you. This is one of the simplest teachings in religion, namely, that Almighty God will be your companion, will stand by you, help you, and see you through.

—Norman Vincent Peale

101

God said, "My presence is always with you,
and I will give you rest."

Exodus 33:14 NASB

A Moment to Refresh

Where can I go from your Spirit? Where can I flee from your presence? If I go up to the heavens, you are there; if I make my bed in the depths, you are there. If I rise on the wings of the dawn, if I settle on the far side of the sea, even there your hand will guide me, your right hand will hold me fast.

Psalm 139:7–10 NIV

Be strong and courageous. Do not be afraid or terrified because of them, for the LORD your God goes with you; he will never leave you nor forsake you.

Deuteronomy 31:6 NIV

O come, let us sing unto the LORD: let us make a joyful noise to the rock of our salvation. Let us come before his presence with thanksgiving, and make a joyful noise unto him with psalms. For the LORD is a great God, and a great King above all gods.

Psalm 95:1–3 KJV

God is above, presiding; beneath, sustaining; within, filling.

—HILDEBERT OF LAVARDIN

Jesus said, "Where two or three come together in my name, there am I with them."

Matthew 18:20 NIV

You have made known to me the path of life; you will fill me with joy in your presence, with eternal pleasures at your right hand.

Psalm 16:11 NIV

We are always in the presence of God.

—D. MARTYN LLOYD-JONES

No one has ever seen God; but if we love one another, God lives in us and his love is made complete in us. We know that we live in him and he in us, because he has given us of his Spirit.

1 John 4:12–13 NIV

As for me, it is good to be near God. I have made the Sovereign Lord my refuge; I will tell of all your deeds.

Psalm 73:28 NIV

The Hard Choice

A Moment to Pause

Close your office door—or find another place free from disruptions—and take a few moments to recall and evaluate choices you recently made in your personal or professional life. Regardless of the impetus or the outcome, choices require courage. Some people think courage is a natural attribute—you either have it or you don't. But this belief is incorrect, because courage is actually a choice anyone can make. It is a choice to go forward with what is right.

As a leader, you must demonstrate the courage to try new things, to make bold changes, to face tough challenges, and to protect your people and your organization. Because of the responsibilities you hold and the decisions you must make, you stand daily at the crossroads of fear and courage.

The path of fear fills your heart with doubts while the path of courage fills your heart with dreams. The path of fear appeals to your desire for safety while the path of courage appeals to your desire for success. Sometimes the choice is hard to make. Yet as anyone who has achieved great things in life can tell you— only the path of courage can be your road to destiny.

Courage is not simply one of the virtues, but the form of every virtue at the testing point.
—C. S. Lewis

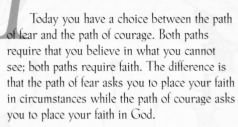

A Moment to Reflect Today you have a choice between the path of fear and the path of courage. Both paths require that you believe in what you cannot see; both paths require faith. The difference is that the path of fear asks you to place your faith in circumstances while the path of courage asks you to place your faith in God.

Courage is putting your faith in God into action. What are the challenges or decisions you face today? Ask God for direction and guidance. Make sure your plans line up with the leadership principles in the Bible. Then be bold. Move forward. Choose courage.

Courage is an inner resolution to go forward in spite of obstacles and frightening situations; cowardice is a submissive surrender to circumstance. Courage faces fear and thereby masters it; cowardice represses fear and is thereby mastered by it. We must constantly build dikes of courage to hold back the flood of fear.

—Martin Luther King Jr.

Be strong and do not lose courage, for there is reward for your work.

2 Chronicles 15:7 NASB

A Moment to Refresh
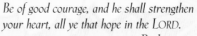

Be of good courage, and he shall strengthen your heart, all ye that hope in the LORD.

Psalm 31:24 KJV

Surely God is my salvation; I will trust and not be afraid. The LORD, the LORD, is my strength and my song; he has become my salvation.

Isaiah 12:2 NIV

There is no fear in love. But perfect love drives out fear, because fear has to do with punishment. The one who fears is not made perfect in love.

1 John 4:18 NIV

Jesus said, "Do not be afraid, little flock, for your Father has been pleased to give you the kingdom."

Luke 12:32 NIV

Courage is the strength or choice to begin a change.
Determination is the persistence to continue in that change.

—Author Unknown

The Spirit that God has given you does not make you slaves and cause you to be afraid; instead, the Spirit makes you God's children, and by the Spirit's power we cry out to God, "Father! my Father!"

Romans 8:15 GNT

The LORD said to Joshua: "Have I not commanded you? Be strong and courageous. Do not be terrified; do not be discouraged, for the LORD your God will be with you wherever you go."

Joshua 1:9 NIV

The LORD is with me; I will not be afraid. What can man do to me? . . . I was pushed back and about to fall, but the LORD helped me. The LORD is my strength and my song; he has become my salvation.

Psalm 118:6, 13–14 NIV

Father, hear the prayer we offer;
Not for ease that prayer shall,
But for strength that we may ever
Live our lives courageously.

—Love Maria Willis

Desire Fulfilled

A Moment to Pause Take time to release tension from your upper body. Roll your shoulders forward and back. Stretch your arms above your head. Reach forward and then arch backward. Roll your head to the right and then to the left. Now put your feet up, lean back, and rest. Enjoy the satisfaction of a moment of relaxation.

Every person has a desire for satisfaction. As a leader, you have a particularly powerful opportunity to make choices that bring satisfaction to your life. In order to find satisfaction, however, you must look beyond your interests and find your passions. The abilities and gifts God gave you are key to discovering those passions. What can you do that you love to do? What endeavors fill you with energy and drive? What causes motivate you to strive and create? What accomplishments fill you with a sense of significance?

The things that motivate you and drive you are not there by coincidence. God has planted them within you. They compose the unique set of traits you need in order to be and do all God has called you to. When God plants a desire within your heart, he intends to fulfill it. The desire is there to help you find his path and his purposes for your life.

Desire only God, and your heart
will be satisfied.
—SAINT AUGUSTINE OF HIPPO

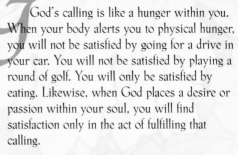

A Moment to Reflect

God's calling is like a hunger within you. When your body alerts you to physical hunger, you will not be satisfied by going for a drive in your car. You will not be satisfied by playing a round of golf. You will only be satisfied by eating. Likewise, when God places a desire or passion within your soul, you will find satisfaction only in the act of fulfilling that calling.

Ask God to help you discover the answers to the questions above. What place do your specific abilities and passions have within your company? Use your insights to help you prioritize and choose how you will spend your time and energy this week. Satisfaction is waiting, and it's within you.

My Son, I must be thy Supreme and final end, if thou desirest to be truly happy. It is I who gave thee all. So look upon each blessing as flowing from the Supreme Good, and thus all things are to be attributed to Me as their source.

—THOMAS À KEMPIS

He satisfies the thirsty and fills the hungry with good things.

—Psalm 107:9 NIV

A Moment to Refresh

The LORD will guide you always; he will satisfy your needs in a sun-scorched land and will strengthen your frame. You will be like a well-watered garden, like a spring whose waters never fail.

Isaiah 58:11 NIV

"I will fill the soul of the priests with abundance, and my people shall be satisfied with My goodness," declares the LORD.

Jeremiah 31:14 NASB

Delight yourself in the LORD and he will give you the desires of your heart. Commit your way to the LORD; trust in him, and he will do this.

Psalm 37:4–5 NIV

The enjoyment of God is the only happiness with which our souls can be satisfied.

ॐ

—JOHN EDWARDS

The fear of the LORD leads to life, so that one may sleep satisfied, untouched by evil.
Proverbs 19:23 NASB

You open your hand and satisfy the desires of every living thing.
Psalm 145:16 NIV

Whom have I in heaven but you, O LORD? And earth has nothing I desire besides you.
Psalm 73:25 NIV

Jesus said, "Blessed are those who hunger and thirst for righteousness, for they shall be satisfied."
Matthew 5:6 NASB

You have made us for yourself and our hearts are restless until they find their rest in you.

ॐ

—SAINT AUGUSTINE OF HIPPO

Weightlifters

A Moment to Pause

Locate a quiet place with a comfortable, high-backed chair. Lean back and rest against the back of the chair so your head's weight is no longer carried by your shoulders. Take several deep, slow breaths, letting tension lift from your shoulders each time you exhale. Use these moments to recall the people whose words encourage you in your work and affirm confidence in your leadership. Like the high-backed chair in which you rest, these words offer support and help lift the weight of responsibility from your shoulders.

Because you are a leader, your kind words also have particular power. Learn to use that power to lift the weight of hesitancy or insecurity from those you lead. Build their confidence, and strengthen their resolve. Flame their good ideas into great ones.

Kind words often become self-fulfilling prophecies. They make it easier for people to attain their goals and live up to all they can be. They motivate people to reach for more. Use your words to acknowledge the good in other people. Recognize their potential and draw out their gifts. They will strive to live up to your comments. They will benefit, and your organization will benefit as well.

Kind words produce their image on men's souls;
and a beautiful image it is. They smooth, and
quiet, and comfort the hearer.
—BLAISE PASCAL

A Moment to Reflect

The book of Proverbs says that life and death are in the power of the tongue. You have the ability to choose life each day; not only for yourself, but also for those you lead. Begin today to weigh your words. Consider how a person's life might change if he hears one kind or encouraging comment from you each week.

Your words have value. They are actually an investment in the lives of others. Determine specific people who need to hear kind words from you today. You can be confident that one day you will receive back your investment, with dividends.

Lord, if words can wound,
Can they not as well heal?
Can they not as well restore?
Can they not as well empower?
Take my words this day and use them
as an ointment when souls ache,
as a mortar when plans crumble,
as a life surge when strength ebbs.

—MELINDA MAHAND

113

*An anxious heart weighs a man down, but a
kind word cheers him up.*

Proverbs 12:25 NIV

A Moment to Refresh

*We don't put anything in anyone's way. So no
one can find fault with our work for God.
Instead, we make it clear that we serve God in
every way. We serve him by holding steady. We
stand firm in all kinds of troubles, hard times
and suffering . . . We remain pure. We
understand completely what it means to serve
God. We are patient and kind. We serve him in
the power of the Holy Spirit. We serve him with
true love.*

2 Corinthians 6:3–4, 6 NIRV

*A man finds joy in giving an apt reply—and
how good is a timely word!*

Proverbs 15:23 NIV

*We always speak as God wants us to, because
he has judged us worthy to be entrusted with the
Good News. We do not try to please people,
but to please God, who tests our motives.*

1 Thessalonians 2:4 GNT

Kind words can be short and easy to speak,
but their echoes are truly endless.

⌇

—MOTHER TERESA

Pleasant words are a honeycomb, sweet to
the soul and healing to the bones.
Proverbs 16:24 NIV

May my lips pour out praise to you
because you teach me your orders. May my
tongue sing about your word, because all of
your commands are right.
Psalm 119:171–172 NIRV

A man of knowledge uses words with
restraint, and a man of understanding is
even-tempered.
Proverbs 17:27 NIV

The mouth of the righteous man utters
wisdom, and his tongue speaks what is just.
Psalm 37:30 NIV

Take my lips and let
them be
Filled with messages
from Thee.

⌇

—FRANCES RIDLEY
HAVERGAL

Made of Bedrock

Step away from the responsibilities of your office for a short while. Find a quiet place to relax and spend the time conversing with God about the things that are on your mind today. Remember that listening is a crucial component of any conversation. As you listen, you can have confidence that God's guidance will be true and right. It will also be consistent with the message he gave in Scripture, because he is a God of integrity. His example is a good model for your own life, because as a leader, you too must possess integrity of heart.

Integrity is honesty, incorruptibility, the quality of being undivided. A person of integrity recognizes that his word matters and that his honor is rooted in his commitment to fulfilling his responsibilities. When you exemplify integrity, other people can have bedrock certainty that you will be there, doing your part and keeping your word, because you are trustworthy.

Your reputation for integrity is a crucial component of every conversation you have and every deal you make. Be dependable. Keep promises. Be on time. Fulfill your obligations. People may question your idea, your decision, or your plan, but they must never have cause to question your integrity.

Integrity is the noblest possession.

—LATIN PROVERB

A Moment to Reflect

Integrity reveals itself in three levels of relationships. First, your boss or stockholders must be able to stake their reputation on your integrity. Second, your personal support system must also be composed of people who exemplify integrity, so that your reputation will not be marred by the behaviors of others.

Finally, those you lead need to know what to expect from you. They need to know you will not change with the mood or the circumstances of the day. Leaders need to know they can count on you. When you have integrity, others have faith in your words and actions and are therefore willing to follow.

Honesty has a beautiful and refreshing simplicity about it. No ulterior motives. No hidden meanings. An absence of hypocrisy, duplicity, political games, and verbal superficiality. As honesty and real integrity characterize our lives, there will be no need to manipulate others

—CHARLES R. SWINDOLL

*Vindicate me, O LORD, for I have walked in
my integrity, and I have trusted in the LORD
without wavering.*

Psalm 26:1 NASB

A Moment to Refresh

*Remember now, O LORD, I beseech You, how I
have walked before You in truth and with a
whole heart and have done what is good in
Your sight.*

2 Kings 20:3 NASB

*The man of integrity walks securely, but he who
takes crooked paths will be found out.*

Proverbs 10:9 NIV

*As for me, I shall walk in my integrity; redeem
me, and be gracious to me.*

Psalm 26:11 NASB

*Better is a poor man who walks in his integrity
than he who is perverse in speech and is a fool.*

Proverbs 19:1 NASB

*Let everything you do relect the integrity and
seriousness of your teaching.*

Titus 2:7 NIV

Integrity of heart is indispensable.

—JOHN CALVIN

O LORD, who may abide in Your tent?
Who may dwell on Your holy hill? He who
walks with integrity, and works
righteousness, and speaks truth in his heart.
He does not slander with his tongue, nor
does evil to his neighbor, nor takes up a
reproach against his friend; in whose eyes a
reprobate is despised, but who honors those
who fear the LORD; he swears to his own
hurt and does not change.

Psalm 15:1–4 NASB

Your love is always with me. I have always
lived by your truth. I don't spend time with
people who tell lies. I don't keep company
with pretenders.

Psalm 26:3–4 NIRV

He who pursues righteousness and love
finds life, prosperity and honor.

Proverbs 21:21 NIV

He is rich or poor
according to what
he is, not according
to what he has.

—HENRY WARD
BEECHER

Finding a Fresh Start

A Moment to Pause   Take a break from the endeavors that have claimed your energy and attention today. Spend this time enjoying a cup of coffee, a brief walk outdoors, a few minutes of simple rest, or whatever other change of pace will help you restore your focus and give you a fresh start to approaching today's tasks. A fresh start renews perspective, cultivates optimism, and multiplies possibilities. A fresh start is often crucial in order to attain challenging goals.

God understands the importance of a fresh start. When you fail in some area, he is ready to help you begin again. He is always nearby, offering grace and forgiveness. As you seek to get back on track, accepting his forgiveness is an all-important step to take for several reasons.

First, accepting forgiveness helps you set your sight on the future. You can look toward what is new. You can operate from a position of optimism. Second, accepting forgiveness sets you free from the trap of blaming others. It allows you to spend your energy minimizing the damage and moving past it. Finally, accepting forgiveness is the impetus that gets you moving forward again. And in business as in life, moving forward again is the key to ultimately achieving success.

The most marvelous ingredient in the forgiveness of God is that he also forgets.
—OSWALD CHAMBERS

A Moment to Reflect

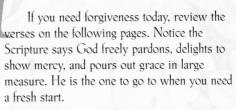

If you need forgiveness today, review the verses on the following pages. Notice the Scripture says God freely pardons, delights to show mercy, and pours out grace in large measure. He is the one to go to when you need a fresh start.

Pray these verses as your personal words of request and words of praise to God. Claim the forgiveness he offers. Then get up and move on. Don't let the past keep you from the victory of the future. Instead, let your fresh start motivate you to work harder, remain truer, and reach higher.

Dark is the stain that we cannot hide—
What can avail to wash it away?
Look! there is flowing a crimson tide—
Whiter than snow you may be today.
Grace, grace, God's grace,
Grace that will pardon and cleanse within,
Grace, grace, God's grace,
Grace that is greater than all our sin!

—JULIA H. JOHNSTON

If we confess our sins, he is faithful and just
and will forgive us our sins and purify us from
all unrighteousness.

1 John 1:9 NIV

A Moment to Refresh

The LORD's lovingkindnesses indeed never
cease, for His compassions never fail. They are
new every morning; great is Your faithfulness.

Lamentations 3:22–23 NASB

As high as the heavens are above the earth, so
great is his love for those who fear him; as far
as the east is from the west, so far has he
removed our transgressions from us.

Psalm 103:11–12 NIV

By the blood of Christ we are set free, that is,
our sins are forgiven. How great is the grace of
God, which he gave to us in such large
measure!

Ephesians 1:7–8 GNT

LORD, suppose you kept a record of sins. Lord,
who then wouldn't be found guilty? But you
forgive. So people have respect for you.

Psalm 130:3–4 NIRV

I think that if God forgives us, we must forgive ourselves.

—C. S. Lewis

Have mercy on me, O Lord, for I call to you all day long. Bring joy to your servant, for to you, O Lord, I lift up my soul. You are forgiving and good, O Lord, abounding in love to all who call to you. Hear my prayer, O LORD; listen to my cry for mercy. In the day of my trouble I will call to you, for you will answer me.

Psalm 86:3–7 NIV

Who is a God like you, who pardons sin and forgives the transgression of the remnant of his inheritance? You do not stay angry forever but delight to show mercy. You will again have compassion on us; you will tread our sins underfoot and hurl all our iniquities into the depths of the sea.

Micah 7:18–19 NIV

In these days of guilt complexes, perhaps the most glorious word in the English language is "forgiveness."

—Billy Graham

Multiplied Blessing

A Moment to Pause

Claim some time for yourself today. Spend a few minutes alone talking to God or meditating on a Bible verse that has helped you recently. Recognize that this time is an investment in yourself and that it has the potential to give ample return to both you and your company. As a leader, how you invest your time, your energy, your influence, and your money is of utmost importance. Each of these items is a limited resource. Your challenge is to identify where they are best invested and where they will bring a multiplied return and a multiplied blessing.

When there is expenditure within your organization, you know there will be a debit on the company's ledger. Yet you also understand the nature of investing. You know that right expenditures bring about future profit, not loss. Expenditures in other aspects of your life work the same way. When you spend your time, energy, and money on the right people and right endeavors, your expenditure actually becomes an investment. Good investments ultimately result in bountiful returns.

Learn to value the resources God has provided. Consider each of them to be like a grain of corn—once planted and cultivated, that one seed will produce fruit that contains multiple grain.

We make a living by what we get. We make a life by what we give.
—DUANE HULSE

A Moment to Reflect

Your leadership responsibilities put you in constant contact with people who would like you to contribute to their enterprises and participate in their projects. Evaluate the invitations you have recently received to invest in another person, organization, or endeavor. Consider where to best invest your time, your talent, your money, and your commitment.

Seek God's guidance as you make decisions regarding where to spend your resources. He has honored you with many blessings. Thank him for the opportunity to multiply and share those blessings by investing in others. Learn to see giving as he does—not as subtraction, but as multiplication.

The seed that is sown is scattered with an open hand. The sower in order to have a harvest has to turn loose the seed. He can't grip it in his fist; he can't hesitate to let it go; he can't just sprinkle a little bit her and there—he's got to let it go and let it go liberally, if he expects to have a great harvest.

—CHARLES H. SPURGEON

125

A generous man will prosper; he who refreshes
others will himself be refreshed.

Proverbs 11:25 NIV

A Moment to Refresh

Cast your bread upon the waters, for after
many days you will find it again.

Ecclesiastes 11:1 NIV

In everything I did, I showed you that by this
kind of hard work we must help the weak,
remembering the words the Lord Jesus himself
said: "It is more blessed to give than to receive."

Acts 20:35 NIV

Remember this: Whoever sows sparingly will
also reap sparingly, and whoever sows
generously will also reap generously. Each man
should give what he has decided in his heart to
give, not reluctantly or under compulsion, for
God loves a cheerful giver. And God is able to
make all grace abound to you, so that in all
things at all times, having all that you need, you
will abound in every good work.

2 Corinthians 9:6–8 NIV

In this world, it is not what we take up but what we give up that makes us rich.

—Henry Ward Beecher

Jesus saw the rich putting their gifts into the temple treasury. He also saw a poor widow put in two very small copper coins. "I tell you the truth," he said, "this poor widow has put in more than all the others. All these people gave their gifts out of their wealth; but she out of her poverty put in all she had to live on."

Luke 21:1–4 NIV

We are never more like God than when we give.

—Charles R. Swindoll

A gift opens the way for the one who gives it. It helps him meet important people

Proverbs 18:16 NIRV

Freely you have received, freely give.

Matthew 10:8 NIV

A secret gift calms anger down. A hidden favor softens great anger.

Proverbs 21:14 NIRV

At Inspirio we love to hear from you—your
stories, your feedback,
and your product ideas.
Please send your comments to us
by way of e-mail at
icares@zondervan.com
or to the address below:

inspirio

Attn: Inspirio Cares
5300 Patterson Avenue SE
Grand Rapids, MI 49530

If you would like further information
about Inspirio and the products we
create please visit us at:
www.inspiriogifts.com

Thank you and God Bless!